JOHN DEWEY'S THOUGHT
AND ITS IMPLICATIONS FOR
CHRISTIAN EDUCATION

MANFORD GEORGE GUTZKE

KING'S CROWN PRESS

COLUMBIA UNIVERSITY, NEW YORK 1956

KING'S CROWN PRESS

is an imprint established by Columbia University Press for the purpose of making certain scholarly material available at minimum cost. Toward that end, the publishers have used standardized formats incorporating every reasonable economy that does not interfere with legibility. The author has assumed responsibility for editorial style and for proofreading.

Library of Congress Catalog Card Number: 55-10466

PUBLISHED IN GREAT BRITAIN, CANADA, INDIA,
AND PAKISTAN
BY GEOFFREY CUMBERLEGE: OXFORD
UNIVERSITY PRESS
LONDON, TORONTO, BOMBAY, AND KARACHI

MANUFACTURED IN THE UNITED STATES OF AMERICA

TO MY WIFE

PREFACE

Many persons in modern times have been confused and disturbed by the apparent conflict between "science" and "religion." Christianity looms in history as the greatest single sustained movement the world has ever seen. Modern science has produced results so self-evident and so impressive that its prestige seems to overshadow any other possible mode of consciousness. With a soul that seeks assurance and comfort, and a mind that craves knowledge and understanding, the candid individual has been baffled to know which approach to follow. It has been popular to assume that a man could have more "faith" if he had a less inquiring mind, and that as he gained more "knowledge" he would by that much believe less. From such an outlook the person who affirmed confidence in the Bible as authentic revelation of truth, not to be otherwise known, was named "obscurantist," and the person who was intellectually educated was not expected to be able to "accept" the historic tenets of Christian faith. This situation has not only caused much distress, but it has misled many honest persons into a prejudice against the Gospel which has left them in lonely darkness, with poverty of soul and bondage of spirit as they face the issues of virtue and destiny.

The study set forth in this book has been developed from the point of view that no real conflict exists between "Western science" and "Christian faith." This is not to deny that there have been conflicts between "scientists" and "theologians," but it is to say that such conflict was not necessary or implicit. The very fact that there are competent "scientists" who affirm their acceptance of Biblical doctrines, and that there are devout Christians who pursue scientific research, supports the point of view of the argument of this treatise.

Further, the study has been developed within the framework of the contemporary intellectual situation. Educational techniques in secondary schools employ and emphasize the scientific approach with the result that the common mind is cast along the lines of modern science. This is not to be deplored, but to be recognized. Any attempt to teach the Christian Gospel today would promise greater success as it employed scientific method.

The average congregation is composed of persons educated in modern schools. The minds of such persons are not only trained to think "scientifically" but are conditioned to accept what is set forth in scientific fashion, and to reject what is presented in the form of tradition. That such a mind is liable to miss much of what is enriching and ennobling in the heritage of the ages is beside the point. It is the only mind such persons have. It is to that mind the Gospel must be presented. The inspiration for the research into educational principles which is the background of this discussion was the burden of concern to discover whether a scientific presentation of the Christian Gospel is feasible. In other words, could the historic message of Jesus Christ as set forth in the Scriptures be effectively presented to a mind that has been cultured in the mood and mode of modern science? Would it be necessary to disparage science, at the risk of alienating the hearers? Or would it be necessary to modify the Gospel, at the risk of deceiving the people? The ramifications of this issue so raised extend far beyond the scope of this study, but this examination of the thought of a notable modern educational philosopher in its

bearing upon the problem of education in religion has been undertaken as one project of exploration. The discussion as written is designed as a demonstration of the validity of the thesis that the method of experimental science can be properly and profitably employed in the propagation of the Christian Gospel.

It will be important to keep in mind that "science" as a mode of dealing with things as events is not to be limited to physical subject matter. The characteristic procedure of science is applicable to problems of the heart as well as the intellect. Also, it will help to avoid misunderstanding to note that "nature" does not designate merely one class of inanimate things, but rather the relational aspect of anything. This meaning of the term is grounded in the general reference to "the nature of," in the sense that attention is focused upon relationship. Thus it would be proper to refer to the nature of soul, the nature of spirit, the nature of God, etc., so that "natural science" is not to be limited to the physical. In fact it is not to be limited at all as to subject matter, but is to be understood as dealing with the relational aspect of whatever is being considered.

It will be essential that the reader grasp and hold in mind always the specific meanings of the terms "instrumental" and "final." This will give insight above all else into Deweyan thinking about anything. At the risk of being tedious, but for the sake of any reader not versed in Dewey's terminology, a brief explanation of the use of these words is given here. Any thing, or any event, has both "instrumental" and "final" aspects. When reference is made to causal relations, that is, when the attention is focused upon what preceded, what else is involved, and what follows or may follow as result, the term "instrumental" is used. The thing is being viewed as an "instrument" in the course of events. When reference is made to the thing itself, to the immediate occurrence of that thing as an event, to the joy, the sorrow, the pleasure, the pain, the sensations, etc., incidental to the experience of that event, the term "final" is used. Whatever constitutes the event is all there is to it, it is "final" in the sense there is nothing else, there is no more than that, in the event itself. Generally speaking, the intellect deals with the "instrumental," whereas the heart cherishes the "final." Thus the "instrumental" is abstract, while the "final" is concrete. The "instrumental" is the ground for the operations of science, but the "final" gives value and worth to that which is being dealt with by science. Dewey would be the first to warn against the fallacy of holding the "instrumental" as being of greater significance. Within the technical scope of scientific procedure the "instrumental" is not so much superior as basic and essential, but in the larger concerns of living and being the "instrumental" is secondary to the "final." The skill, the techniques of the surgeon are "instrumental," but the baby alive in your arms is "final." With all due respect to the surgeon, what really counts with you is the baby. In some such way "science" and "religion" are to be seen as dealing with the "instrumental" and the "final" aspects of reality. Dewey's philosophic preoccupation with the "instrumental" elements in the knowledge process has earned the designation of "instrumentalism" in reference to his system of thinking, but he has never failed to remind his readers that all value and worth is grounded in the "final" phases of experience.

This study was begun as research to explore the possibility and the consequence of utilizing the operation of intelligence in the deliberate propagation of the Christian message and the culture of Christian religious experience. The term "Christian" is lifted originally from the literature of the New Testament where it is used as a *noun,* designating a specific class of persons. When it is used in this dis-

cussion as an *adjective* it is intended to denote traits and characteristics belonging specifically to such persons as described in the New Testament, viz., "The disciples were called Christians first at Antioch." The "Christian message" is taken to be the historic presentation of that which the New Testament records as the doctrine of the apostles in the beginnings of the history of the Christian Church. Grounded in certain specific historical events reported by eyewitnesses, and interpreted by certain men accepted as true apostles, a core of Christian doctrine is set forth in the New Testament, which is taken as the content of Christian faith. These tenets include the unchangeable nature of God, the omnipotent sovereignty of God which enables Him to control and to manipulate events at His will, the unique significance of the Incarnation, the unalterable meaning of the Crucifixion, the reality of the Resurrection, the present ministry of the living Lord in heaven, the necessity of regeneration, and the eventual activation of God's eternal purpose. When such ideas are "believed" a certain spiritual experience is had, with certain values immediately consummated and certain results in culture directly produced. The enhancing of this experience and the producing of such cultural and practical consequences is the aim of education in Christian religion. It is the conviction of the author that the use of experimental intelligence is both possible and profitable in such educational effort.

The close connection between the ideas set forth in this discussion and the writings of John Dewey, as indicated by the many quotations, is designed to demonstrate that inasmuch as experimental philosophy is grounded in the processes of nature, it can be utilized without alteration or discount in the understanding of the processes of Christian education. The basic ideas appear obvious: Christians are men, men are in nature; and experimental philosophy is

grounded in nature. Thus it would seem to follow simply
and clearly that the insights of experimentalism could be
valid in the educational procedures devised and promoted
by Christians to produce Christians. The reader is urged
to be patient when the argument becomes tedious because
of detailed analysis and involved interpretation. This material was prepared as a doctoral dissertation and the argument set forth seemed to demand all possible support by
direct appeal to the works of John Dewey so that there
could be no valid reason to doubt the authenticity of the
discussion which intends to show that the insights Dewey
has set forth are applicable to the problems of education in
religion, even in the Christian religion.

Readers who have personal faith in God as He is revealed
in the Gospel of Jesus Christ may be unsatisfied at times
with the absence of specific affirmations as to the form and
content of Christian faith. Such are asked to keep in mind
the intellectual character of this presentation. The author
cherishes personal convictions grounded in the Scriptures
which he holds to be "the infallible guide and rule in matters of faith and practice." This study is not a matter of
describing faith or practice, but is definitely focused upon
the problem of understanding aspects of the educational
process. There are principles involved in the process in
which men learn, some of which have been effectively described and elaborated in the philosophy of experimentalism, eminently set forth by John Dewey, which have now
become incorporated in contemporary educational techniques, and so are known and familiar to the people of our
time. This study aims to point out that such principles are
also operative in education in religion, and their use would
contribute to the effectiveness of Christian education today.
The matter of the content of faith is not an indifferent affair,
but it is not the matter in hand in this discussion.

Technical skill can produce a steel blade of most excellent quality, but it has no bearing on the use which may be made of its product. That blade may be a surgeon's scalpel or an assassin's stiletto. There is nothing in the process of production that will determine the final consequence to mankind. But the skill can be used to advantage to improve the surgeon's equipment for the saving of human life. This analogy points to the author's approach to experimentalism. This contemporary mode of observation and study is directly grounded in and related to natural processes of any and every sort. Its competence is available for use in the propagation of Christian ideas to the welfare of all men.

Acknowledgment of help and encouragement received in the preparation of the manuscript will necessarily be inadequate and incomplete. This material has been discussed with many who have contributed insight, criticism, and encouragement whose names cannot be given here. Yet, it would be much less than proper not to mention the members of the Faculty of Columbia University who guided my research and who have read and criticized the manuscript in its preparation. F. Ernest Johnson, as faculty adviser; R. Bruce Raup, as Chairman of my Dissertation Committee until the last year before its final acceptance; John R. Childs, as Acting-Chairman succeeding Prof. Raup, and a helpful critic of the dissertation in its preparation (all of the Department of Philosophical Foundations in Teacher's College); and Horace E. Friess, of the Department of Philosophy in Columbia University, constituted the committee who patiently and carefully checked the philosophical soundness and academic quality of the material now incorporated in this book. I shall always be humbly indebted to these scholars for their help and for their professional candor in granting me personally the freedom to point my discussion to the end in which I was primarily interested.

and as a Minister of the Gospel in a busy program of preaching and teaching. I am indebted to President J. McDowell Richards for his constant interest and steady encouragement, and to many others whose names I cannot begin to list here, whose interest has been an inspiration and whose confidence in the validity of my argument has been a challenge.

MANFORD GEO. GUTZKE

October, 1955

Any public expression of my indebtedness to my wife will be woefully inadequate. Her interest in this problem, her patient support in my long program of study and research, her intelligent discernment in the matters discussed, her constant encouragement throughout the tedious years of preparation of this material, together with her helpful suggestions and her unfaltering confidence in the significance of the work, have amounted to a measure of contribution that cannot be overestimated.

Many friends have given encouragement to the project of publishing this book. Substantial aid in financing the project was given by the Shenandoah Presbyterian Church of Miami, Florida, by the Monday Night Bible Class of North Avenue Presbyterian Church of Atlanta, Georgia, and by Mr. Winfield Morten of Dallas, Texas.

Permission to quote from copyrighted publications was graciously given by the following, to whom the proper acknowledgment and appreciation of favor granted is due: The Tudor Publishing Company of New York for permission to quote from the *Library of Living Philosophers*, Volume I: *The Philosophy of John Dewey*, Paul Schilpp, editor; G. P. Putnam's Sons of New York, for permission to quote from three published works of John Dewey: *Art as Experience*, *The Quest for Certainty*, and *Philosophy and Civilization*; Henry Holt and Company, Inc., of New York, for permission to quote from *Human Nature and Conduct* by John Dewey, and *Ethics* by Dewey and Tufts; D. C. Heath and Company of Boston, Massachusetts, for permission to quote from *How We Think* by John Dewey; The Philosophical Library of New York, for permission to quote from *Problems of Men* by John Dewey.

The work of research, study, and preparation of this material has been carried on while I have served as a member of the faculty of Columbia Theological Seminary

CONTENTS

I: INTRODUCTION

The fortunes and welfare of men in the modern world have been significantly and profoundly affected by the adoption of a unique and distinct approach to the problems of living, known as Science. By noting intrinsic causal relations in sequential events, so that elements necessary for the eventual better and greater were looked for in the present and the actual, the genius of a new philosophic temper and approach to the affairs of men was manifested. There was now a reluctance to make assumptions, an unwillingness to "take for granted," or to accept the "given," while every respect was shown for empirical data, and it was emphasized that concrete events as they actually occurred should be carefully observed. Techniques of controlled, directed observation were developed with increasing efficiency as experimentation was fostered. The apparent validity of such procedures in discovering the true nature of reality on the basis of what was actually happening in the world grounded a new philosophic mood, known as the pragmatic. This, in turn, inspired a bold reconstruction in intellectual outlook, in correlation with the expanding application of the new methodology in handling practical affairs. At the same time there was a growing intellectual interest everywhere in the problem of human welfare. Out of this welter of shifting viewpoint and changing interest has emerged the contemporary philosophy called "Experimentalism."

Within this system of thought, man is considered as being primarily and essentially a creature whose needs are supplied and whose values are found in his interactions with his environment. Consequently, the biological serves readily as one important mode of interpretation of human affairs, and functional categories are preferred in interpreting the significance of all that concerns man. It is not exactly claimed that such are the only intellectual possibilities, but they are held as eminently suitable to serve our practical interests: a fact which has been especially congenial to our cultural character as Americans. Corroboration of this judgment seems abundantly evident, since any form of deliberate activity which is promoted as the basis of such an experimental approach to the problem in hand is by that much more likely to prove effectual. Thus, humane considerations alone warrant the adoption of this outlook upon the problems of men in a society such as ours where human welfare is accepted as a proper public concern.

This may well account for the readiness and the enthusiasm with which experimentalist theory and technique have been so largely employed in the development of American education. In any case, our great public school system and program has definitely experimentalist elements, and presents impressive demonstration of the validity of the experimental approach in the propagation and dissemination of learning. This in turn has developed and trained the thinking procedures of Americans, so there is commonly abroad amongst us a strong potential predisposition to accept as significant and valid only such considerations as are couched in experimentalist terms. Not the traditional, nor the formal, but the functional, and in that sense the practical, is held to be the vital, the important. Though readily demonstrated in common-sense affairs, this mood is by no means limited to, or even committed to, these practical interests. Cultural, social, personal, and even esthetic problems are approached and handled within the scope of the experimentalist perspective, and seem to be soluble through the application of this method. In the light of these facts, which indicate the virtue and the potentialities of this mode of philosophic thinking for the promotion of human values, the problem with which the ensuing study is concerned may be understood and appreciated. If religion is recognized as an aspect of human experience, so that participation in religious affairs, being something man does, can be learned, would education in religion benefit by the adoption of experimentalist theory and technique? Survey of this problem poses three related questions:

1. Is the philosophy of experimentalism, as set forth by John Dewey, applicable to interpretation of the problem of education in religion?

2. How would it apply in the development of instrumentalities for the promotion of education in religion?

3. What sort of results would follow the application of such experimentalist thinking in education in religion? Since experimentalism has influenced the American mind so significantly through educational techniques, the validity of the experimentalist approach in matters of religion is of prime importance in our life and society today.

The philosophy of experimentalism has been formulated in the interpretation of the procedures of modern science, as "scientific method at last come to self-consciousness," largely in the works of American thinkers, particularly Charles Sanders Peirce, William James, and John Dewey. In addition to his great work in describing its logical structure, and in elaborating its implications in the knowledge process, Dewey has labored to demonstrate the concrete values of experimental inquiry in the handling of all the problems of men. He has not only insisted that experimental method would serve every human interest, but he has affirmed his earnest conviction that such application of practical intelligence is imperative. In one of his later publications he writes:

There are issues in the conduct of human affairs in their production of good and evil which, at a given time and place, are so central, so strategic in position, that their urgency deserves, with respect to practice, the name ultimate and comprehensive. These issues demand the most systematic re-flective attention that can be given. It is relatively unimportant whether this attention be called philosophy or by some other name. It is of immense human importance that it be given, and that it be given by means of the best tested resources that inquiry has at command.[1]

Undoubtedly first place among such "best tested resources" should be given to the insights and procedures which have been achieved in that school of philosophical thought of which Professor Dewey has been for so long the eminent expositor and foremost teacher.

The appearance of a materialistic limitation in the range of this philosophy, as characteristically manifested in its public exposition, which might seem to handicap its utility in dealing with matters of the spirit, is dispelled when it is viewed in terms of the conditions in which it was generated. Experimental science achieved initial and im-pressive success in the realm of the physical. It followed as a matter of course that when experimentalist thinkers drew upon the so-called natural sciences for illustration of their ideas, there appeared a preponderant list toward the "material" in their frame of reference with a concomitant tendency to ignore and even to devitalize other aspects of experience. Dewey found this cultural cleavage in his philosophic heritage, but his own thinking seems generally free from any such materialistic tropism. It belongs to the competence of his philosophic outlook that while pursuing the experimentalist approach he has achieved full balance

of vision, which may not always be manifest in the body of his works, but which he never fails to display at points of departure and moments of summarization in the course of his thought. That he is conscious of the need of extending philosophic inquiry is clearly expressed in this passage:

Another phase of the present state of philosophy demands notice . . . . It affirms that the purpose and business of philosophy is wholly with that part of the historic tradition called search for wisdom—namely, search for the ends and values that give direction to our collective human activities. It holds that not grasp of eternal and universal Reality but use of the methods and conclusions of our best knowledge, that called scientific, provides the means for conducting this search. It holds that limitations which now exist in this use are to be removed by means of extension of the ways of tested knowing that define science from physical and physiological matters to social and distinctly human affairs. The movement is called, in its various aspects, by the names of pragmatism, experimentalism, instrumentalism. Not these names are important but the ideas that are held regarding the distinctive aim and business of philosophic inquiry and of how it should be accomplished.[*]

He goes on to say even more pointedly with respect to the outlook for experimentalism:

It holds that the scientific method of inquiry has not begun to reach maturity. It holds that it will achieve manhood only when its use is extended to cover all aspects of all matters of human concern. It holds that many of the remediable evils of the present time are due to the unbalanced, one-sided application of the methods of inquiry and test that constitute everything that has a right to the name "science."[3]

To understand fully Dewey's works, which deal obviously with problems stated in secular terms, in the light of such clear expression of his own general judgment, it is helpful to remember that his earlier theoretical labors were performed in the field of education, oriented particularly in the practical problems of American public school education. Here he has been confronted with an arbitrary convention grounded in political and social conditions, which has proscribed attention to religion in the educational program of the state. The situation in which he worked has accordingly been distinctly secular, and so there is inevitably an obvious secularistic tinge in the formulation of his ideas. But Dewey has never admitted the intrinsic validity of such segmentation of human interest. However he may have accepted this circumstance as a fortuitous opportunity to press for a united public support for an enlightened educational program in the face of hopeless divisions existing in the religious phase of American life, he has repudiated and resisted with every means at his command the correlated insinuation of the idea of essential disunity in human nature and experience as would be suggested by the terms sacred and secular.

Dewey makes no claim to have exhausted, in the course of his extensive labors, the apparently infinite resources of the experimental approach, nor to have traced out in any total measure the endless ramifications of its implications, but his basic belief in continuity throughout all-inclusive nature is so settled that he has no doubt as to the universal validity of the ideas which have been conceived within its perspective. His conception of intelligence as the determinative factor in the efficient direction of human affairs may be taken as representative of his philosophical thinking, and he would have no doubt that intelligence is so intrinsically natural that it is potential and actual wherever men live.

This study has been prepared with the main thesis that Dewey's emphasis on the role of intelligence in all aspects of human experience is fundamentally sound, and that the theory of intelligence set forth in his works is applicable

in the problems of religious experience. Professor Dewey has not worked systematically in this latter field, but he has repeatedly emphasized both the possibility and the importance of such extension of experimentalist thought.

Apparently Dewey felt that despite the orientation of his philosophic labors in other directions, he has made significant reference to the religious phase of life, as this excerpt from his rejoinder in Schilpp's volume seems to imply:

I think something could be fruitfully said concerning my philosophic interpretation of experience in its religious aspect.[4]

While this study may not achieve that possibility in the sense Professor Dewey had in mind, it will undertake to set forth a description of some implications of his philosophy which will provide a degree of understanding of what is involved in the exercise of intelligence in the course of religious experience. What is in mind is well set forth in the following report by John Herman Randall, Jr.:

There are two quite different ways of using a method that is essentially critical, two ways well illustrated by two students whom Dewey has taught. One, a brilliant Chinese, despite the fact that Chinese thought exhibits much of the temper of Dewey himself, took Dewey's experimentalism to mean that the slate must be wiped clean for a fresh start. The Chinese part was utterly mistaken, and must be forgotten: men must build anew from scratch, and by assiduous cultivation of the scientific method, develop for China a philosophy embodying all those values which Dewey has found as the permanent deposit of the Christian and individualistic West. The other was a Hindu, confronted by a culture far different from that in which Dewey has operated, and therefore tempted to sweep it too away. But he took the method of Dewey to indicate rather that one should manipulate reflectively the material at one's disposal; and so he tried to arrive at what the peculiar Hindu values might mean

when critically examined in the light of the demands of today.
He emerged, not with the scheme of beliefs which Dewey has
rebuilt for the West, but with a translation of Hindu spirituality
into terms that could stand up in the presence of scientific
criticism. To him Dewey offered a method for dealing with
his own inherited materials. There is little doubt but that he
understood Dewey better than the Chinese, and had a firmer
grasp on the spirit of his experimentalism. For he knew that
Dewey meant not destruction but reconstruction; he knew that
criticism demands a tradition as the material on which to work.[5]

The work of the young Hindu involved the use of intelligence in education in religion. It is the purpose of this
study to examine some of the ideas which would contribute
to an understanding of the procedures employed in such
use of intelligence.

Several assumptions are basic in the thought set forth in
this discussion. The unity of all human experience is inherent in the identity of the individual, who is doing and
undergoing whatever is being experienced; so that despite
the multiform differentiations which may appear in the
course of his conduct there is a simple organum to be held
as the vital center of behavior. While the possibility of
disorder in the personality is not denied, the intrinsic
integrity of the one human being is taken as ground for
belief in the continuity of experience and conduct; so that
processes identified and described intellectually as being
manifested in one phase of experience may be counted as
being operative in other phases even though not yet articu-
lated nor defined. Thus, the phenomena of religion in
human affairs, which place religious experience in human
living, imply that the intellectualization of the processes
involved in conscious experience in its religious aspect,
while variant in form, will manifest the same structural
pattern as would the intellectualization of processes in-

volved in conscious experience in its artistic or its scientific aspects. Dewey has discussed with considerable thoroughness both science and art as manifestations of the analytic and the esthetic characters of human experience, respectively. The present discussion is projected on the assumption that religion is likewise a manifestation of a distinctive character of human experience, and thus can be interpreted in the approach of the philosophy of experimentalism.

The significance of religion will be considered in the body of the discussion, but one further observation could well be kept in mind as the whole study is approached. Whatever goods or values there may be in religious experience, inasmuch as such goods and values are actually *had* in the conscious experience of man, they are to be conceived as natural in their manifestation, being events in the course of continuous sequential experience. As unique as their form may be, they will have histories that may be observed. In so far as man *has* these values, he *acts*—and in so far as he acts, the exercise of conscious choice is possible. Thus the application of practical intelligence may be expected to effect the same sort of advantage and benefit in this area of life as it has been shown to occasion in other areas where it has been made the subject of competent and extensive research.

Religion as referred to in this study will be described in terms that will suffice to distinguish this aspect of experience in a general way. In the first of his Terry lectures, *A Common Faith*, Dewey presents a conception of "religion" as distinct from and almost in opposition to the "religious." The use of the term "religion" in this discussion is not predicated upon that conception (in *A Common Faith*), but upon a more radical analysis of human consciousness set out in such works as *Experience and Nature*,

The Quest for Certainty, and *Art as Experience.* The same basic relation is taken to exist between "religious" and "religion" as is held to exist between "scientific" and "science," and "esthetic" and "art." The ground for the concept as used in this paper is laid in Chapter IV, "The Nature of Man," and a full exposition of the term is set forth in Chapter V, "The Meaning of Religion." While cultural and institutional forms of religion may present bewildering confusion and irreconcilable contradictions, it is held that the character of this aspect of experience is sufficiently normative from the natural point of view to permit such treatment to be meaningful. For example, there will be no disposition to set out the content of religious beliefs; but, that beliefs have content, and that such content is acquired in the course of experience, will be noted and will serve to present the problem of *how* such content is acquired, in order to discover the function of practical intelligence in the process. Illustrations as inserted may appear to be derived from one distinctive religious system of beliefs, but nothing more is intended by the use of these concrete materials than the illustration of the particular points under discussion. Likewise, since religious experience is promoted by practical procedures, instrumentalities designed to lead into preferred results will be taken as they may be obvious in the affairs of men, without noting or seeking to evaluate the relative merit of this or that specific procedure in comparison with others. That they all manifest the elemental principle that organic participation grounds the processes of consciousness will be held to point to the importance of employing intelligence in the use of such instrumental procedures for the development and the sharing of religious values.

In seeking to note the use of intelligence in this enrichment of religious experience, certain classic religious pro-

cedures will be examined to discover evidence of the operation of intelligence. Taking the findings of such examination as a basis, there will then be formulated some tentative proposals for the application of intelligence in contemporary practices devised to promote religious experience. It will be noted that intelligence will be operative not only in designing procedures appropriate to the results desired but in noting the actual empirical events that follow the deliberate use of such instrumentalities, and in reflecting upon the evidence of efficiency or inefficiency, with consequent revision of such procedures to meet changing conditions and to incorporate better understanding and newer insights.

The significance of this whole study will rest upon the soundness of the view that learning is grounded in actual organic participation in practical situations, so that educational procedures are best designed to involve participation by the learner. The comparative esteem accorded to religious values will constitute the basis of the relative importance of such a study; but the validity of the conclusions will demonstrate something of the adequacy of the philosophy of experimentalism to deal with the problems of men.

II: THE PHILOSOPHY OF
JOHN DEWEY

An authentic understanding of the philosophy of John Dewey requires recognition of the point of view from which his approach is made and of the intellectual context within which his conceptions are formulated. Dewey conceived philosophy as intellectual activity related directly to the deliberate resolution of problematic situations arising in the course of human experience. Its vital significance for him is its function in furthering the welfare and fortunes of men. It belongs to Dewey's general outlook that philosophy is not to be pursued as a search for final truth, especially for reality in any fixed form or ultimate being. New discoveries of fact, new inventions in technique, new light from fresh insight, as these occur in the course of events in a changing developing world, will of themselves by their very significance make reconstructions in prior findings necessary. Thus it follows that formulations of conclusions reached in philosophic reflection are in need of constant revision. Hence complete uniformity of expression in the thought of any philosopher over a period of time is not to be expected, either as to form or as to content. Such sameness would indicate a mind out of touch with vital affairs, unrelated to living problems. Dewey is certainly not to be counted among those who busy themselves to maintain formal consistency of expression in a world that is featured by the continuous emergence of novel conditions. However, there is a distinctive character, a recognizable and perduring structure in the thought of Dewey which suffices to give

identity to conceptions which appear in his writings. That character is derived from the intellectual orientation within which Dewey performed his labors.

Dewey goes to the natural sciences for intellectual equipment suited to his purpose of expounding and elaborating the philosophy of experimentalism. While he recognizes science as an unfinished affair, esteeming it still in its infancy, he feels its achievements are sufficiently significant to warrant the adoption of its methods and the acceptance of its findings as the best tested and the best grounded available. His adoption of the basic principles of scientific procedure is a matter of sharing the views held in the intellectual community of which he is an eminent member. He does not hold these beliefs to be fixed, nor does he adopt them uncritically. Nevertheless, they serve as basic assumptions for his thinking and characterize the formulations of his thought. Despite the independent and creative character of his work, Dewey never appears as an enigma, nor as an iconoclast among his contemporaries. Taking what has been established and accepted in his cultural heritage, Dewey labors with great pains to advance the understanding of his fellow men along the lines of his own intellectual insights.

Thus, Dewey's approach to the pattern of experience is set forth in the conceptual context of biological principles. The basic unit is ever man as a living creature in the world of nature. As such, man is entirely in nature and of nature so that all history and every significance of the life of man is held to be altogether natural. It does not belong to the systematic outlook of Dewey's thought to claim this as the finally adequate view; but it seems to be his considered judgment that biological science provides invaluable instrumentalities of language and ideas for the interpretation and understanding of human behavior. At times there appears

an aspect of firm insistence in the use Dewey makes of
biological ideas. The practical instrumental purpose of the
application of these ideas is doubtless always valid from
Dewey's basic philosophical point of view. But the use of
such material places great demand upon the alert attention
of those who follow the argument. It would be doubtless
impractical for an author to insert repeated warnings, such
as might be needed to keep pedestrian minds from making
mistakes in following the turns of thought. Such method
would probably distract, and thus detract from the conceptual impression of the ideas presented, but the necessity for keeping the specific orientation in mind at all times
remains real. This is amply attested by the misunderstand-
ings which have occurred when Dewey's works have been
perused by others, even by men of trained minds. The
adequate safeguard against such error is a simple, sensible
procedure. It is deliberately to keep in mind just the context and just the purpose which Dewey himself has in mind
and has probably indicated in the body of the discussion
with what he deemed sufficient clarity. Dewey's fidelity and
zeal in pursuit of the significance of a particular idea in
a particular situation is so all-absorbing that the ensuing
dislocation of other ideas in other settings that may follow
in the wake of his thorough effort is often decidedly disturbing. What is needed is that every reader should retain a
resolute grasp of the instrumental character of the whole
performance.

This somewhat lengthy observation is pertinent because
of its bearing upon the subsequent study which will be
made of Dewey's conception of intelligence. Intelligence
will be found as described largely within the perspective[1] of
biology, involving the use of ideas which incorporate current biological theory. But current theory in biology includes hypothetical elements conceived at a time when

biological thought was marked by the then prevailing dualism. Hence such ideas may manifest philosophical inadequacies that have not yet been removed by later criticism.[2] And so any study of Dewey's conception of intelligence could easily be confused and diverted because of such philosophical assumptions which may have no actual significance for the particular problem in hand. It would be definitely beside the point to take time to attempt adequate revision by criticism of such unsatisfactory but nonessential incidentals. However, in so passing them by without challenge, there is again the need for vigilance that such ideas be not permitted at the face value of their claims to cause obstruction or perversion to the proposed extension of the implications of intelligence in the study of areas not recognized in the dualism inherent in earlier biological thought. Such caution may well be maintained while being aware that Dewey's acceptance of current biological conceptions is provisional for a practical purpose. His aim is not to set forth biology but to describe and interpret experience. He purposes to do this by employing a specific "universe of discourse," in this case the biological, which he prefers for good and sufficient reasons, and which he would commend to others in all good faith.

A further observation seems in order as the problem of understanding Dewey's philosophy is considered. Just as his language has been noted to be characteristically modish in harmony with his scientific affiliates, so his style of expression presents a somewhat minor problem of hermeneutics. It has been remarked that Dewey's phraseology tends to be cryptic and occasionally misleading because of his custom of using the terms of common speech with specialized meanings. There appears at first glance a deceptive simplicity in his writing. Words used are the common words of everyday speech, but the meanings ascribed to

those words in the text and by the context are quite different
from the common meanings they convey: such words are
invested with meanings defined by Dewey himself, at times
in a very original sense. This practice is doubtless quite
innocent, unless it be designed to suggest and to promote
the revision of common-sense ideas. But it places an onus
of responsibility upon the reader: a task that would have
been made much simpler if Dewey had used such words
consistently in either one or the other sense. Unfortunately,
the practical needs of the particular problem which Dewey
had in hand seem at times to have prevailed in prompting
first this usage and then that. Here again there is no need
that anyone misunderstand. There is simply need for alert
vigilance lest one go astray. It is not always a simple matter
to keep the tremendous scope of Dewey's thoughts in single
perspective, but it is absolutely essential for the understanding of his ideas that the shifting focus of his energetic
intellectual explorations be closely and accurately followed.

Dewey has repeatedly sounded a warning lest the abstract character of scientific conceptions be permitted to
elude the consciousness of those who make use of such
material. He considers the technique of abstraction to be
probably the most significant achievement of the intellect
and is inclined to esteem it as the essential element in
experimental method. But he also holds it to be decidedly
harmful to lose sight of the fact that scientific objects are
abstractions, being constructs of an intellectual procedure
which facilitates the discovery of general facts and thereby
extends the scope of understanding and control to an indefinite degree. In the case of the physical sciences, homogeneity of data is most essential and is secured by the
deliberate selection of the metrical results of physical
operations conducted in investigation of the particular
phenomenon being studied. Such homogeneity, which

makes quantitative treatment and resultant generalizations possible, is the character induced by the method of definition: eminently useful as results have demonstrated, but none the less artificial and instrumental. Absorption of the mind in the discourse of the so-called natural sciences tends to generate the impression that qualitative aspects of experience are insignificant and even unreal. Dewey makes the fallacy of such a view very plain by his clear exposition of the academic nature of scientific thought. Nevertheless this is an admonition which must be taken seriously in the course of examination of Dewey's own ideas. Phrasing his conceptions in the terminology of scientific thought creates this need for careful interpretation when the general significance of his ideas is sought for application in other aspects of experience. It will be maintained in this discussion that scientific method is applicable in the field of religious phenomena, but only when extracted from its ordinary physical and physiological context. Dewey's conceptions must be critically examined to abstract the principles of his insight from the particular formulations in which they have been set forth in the course of his thought.

The foregoing observations do not exhaust every aspect of a sound approach to the interpretation of Dewey's conception of intelligence, but they have been made by way of signaling the purpose of this study to lead the consideration of the significance of Dewey's ideas into aspects of experience which have not been included in the general context of interest in which Dewey himself worked. Dewey does not deny, as much as he may seem to ignore or perhaps even to neglect, the authenticity or the full significance of the religious aspect of experience. But, as has been implied, the standing of the phenomena of religion in the literature of the natural sciences is decidedly precarious, and the attempt to extend Dewey's conceptions formulated in this language into that area requires unusual and painstaking attention to just such and similar aspects in the matter of interpretation as have been indicated above.

It belongs to the practical tenor of Dewey's outlook in his philosophical interest, not only to understand the processes which lead to the having of desired goods, but to recognize how these processes might be utilized and controlled by the individual involved in them. Dewey has pointed out the instrumental significance of knowledge, and has stressed the incalculable advantage to man in the production and use of instrumentalities, "tools," which not only are so helpful to the one who invents and utilizes them but which may be made available to others. The production and employment of such technical structures as will facilitate, increase, and enhance desired results according to the insights and understanding gained in "interpretation" is a second intermediate phase of intellection known as "instrumentation."

Because the knowledge of man is constantly increasing, during which new insights are being had and different conditions are emerging, as well as because the construction of the instrumentality involves the use of abstract ideas with their intrinsic limitations, there is need constantly to check the efficiency of the tool being used, to review the purpose for which it was designed, to experiment with variations and innovations, by way of discovering better structures that will replace outmoded and inadequate "tools." In this the operation of intelligence is a basic factor, and directly related to the fortunes and welfare of men.

Dewey's view of human experience as an integrated whole shows the direct connection between outward physical events and inner conscious events, and provides a basis for understanding that in the manipulation of obvious practical circumstances there may be the clue to the management of those ideal consummations which constitute the values of men. Such outer manipulation of procedures, programs, and participation will employ "instrumentation," which in turn will manifest the operation of intelligence by constant review, revision, and reconstruction to produce more and better results. It is the intellectual grasp of this principle that grounds the facilitation of the operation of intelligence in the promotion of religious experience, i.e., in education in religion.

This element in Dewey's thought has particular import for this study of religious behavior as a mode of mental activity.

The social affords us an observable instance of a "realm of mind" objective to an individual, by entering into which, as a participating member, organic activities are transformed into acts having a mental quality.[3]

That this fitness is obvious even in the very nature of religious consciousness is indicated in the following comment wherein Dewey points the philosophic enterprise into that outlook upon reality which we commonly designate as religious:

It is the historic claim of philosophy that it occupies itself with the ideal of wholes and the whole. It is submitted that either the whole is manifested in concretely empirical ways, and in ways consonant with infinite variety, or else wholeness is but a dialectical speculation. I do not say that the social as we know it *is* the whole, but I do emphatically suggest that it is the widest and richest manifestation of the whole accessible to our observation. As such it is at least the proper point of departure for any more imaginative construings of the whole one may wish to undertake. And in any case it furnishes the terms in which any consistent *empirical* philosophy must speak.[4]

We may expect then that the general tenor of Dewey's philosophy will be congenial to the problems involved in the enhancement and the increase of religious goods. This expectation will be seen to be well grounded when more specific traits of his thinking are noted, as these will now be set forth.

EMPIRICAL

The one condition necessary for any datum to be included in Dewey's outlook is that it must actually have occurred. The nature and meaning of the event is held to

III: THE OPERATION OF
INTELLIGENCE

It belongs to Dewey's whole approach in philosophy to seek explanatory principles in the context of actually experienced events, but this procedure is not as simple as it would seem at first glance. Obviously, a mere succession of discrete sensory events could not comprise the subject matter of sustained intellectual reflection, even if such a succession could exist. Dewey is not ready to concede primary existential status to discrete items, as the "simples" upon which some philosophies depend, since it appears to him they are dialectical constructs taken from the complex matrix of events by intellectual method. For him

there appears to be a fairly straight road to the conclusion that a just gauge of the adequacy of any philosophic account of things is found in the extent to which that account is based upon taking things in the widest and most complex scale of associations open to observation.[1]

In the scale of associations, wherein are recognized "narrower and wider ranges," Dewey takes continuity to be actual, and holds that "the social" "furnishes philosophically the inclusive category on the ground that it is indicative of the widest and richest range of association empirically accessible (and no apology is offered for basing philosophy upon the empirically manifest rather than upon the occult)." Certainly in so far as the subject matter includes meanings, the "social" is the necessary category,

since the mental is empirically discernible only where association is manifested in the form of participation and communication.[2]

be entirely grounded in the actual circumstances of that occurrence. At the same time this condition makes the inclusion of all relevant data mandatory in any responsible investigation. Whatever happens is the primary stuff which can and must be taken into account when there is search for understanding.

The profound import of this empirical element in Dewey's outlook can scarcely be overemphasized. Certainly it is this feature in his thinking which provides the catholic aspect in his intellectual outlook as well as the practical tenor of intelligence, as he conceives it. And it has immediate significance for the discussion in hand. If ever religious experience occurs, it is by that fact authorized to provide data for reflection in the search for wisdom and understanding in the interpretation of the problems of men.

Dewey's discussion of the superiority of the "scientific" over the "empirical" method in *How We Think*,[5] though somewhat confusing in its use of terms, is noteworthy because of its emphasis upon the greater significance for philosophy of the intellectual aspect of subject matter taken for reflection. Empirical data (in his later and more general use of that term) consist not so significantly of sensory reports as such, which would appear in unique, discrete, isolated fashion, as of operational results achieved in controlled exploratory investigation. Noting the singular, unique nature of sensory data, which would tend to render all such data enigmatic in themselves, Dewey points out:

Connection is instituted through operations which define ideas, and operations are as much matters of experience as are sensory qualities.[6]

Thus the direction of operations in investigation is in itself empirical. It is possible for intellection and subject to the operation of intelligence. At this point it may be noted that even though the primary data (sensory in form) should be illusory rather than real, the ideas initiated, developed, formed, and had, would be nonetheless empirical, and so would be valid for philosophical investigation. This observation points to the authenticity of ideas had and held, where the primary data may include that which is spurious or at least questionable. Hence there seems to be no actual limitation of the applicability of this principle which takes the empirical as the ground for all understanding. Apparently it would be valid in religious matters as in any other.

It may further be noted that, in taking empirical data as the proper subject matter for philosophical reflection and study, Dewey not only finds the structure of his ideas in the practical affairs of human living but he makes the practice of philosophy a project that produces human goods. In the empirical method as utilized by science, investigation not only begins with the data of actual experience, but, having reached conclusions as the result of systematic reflection and sustained thought, such conclusions are then returned to actual experience to be verified and employed there in the everyday "macroscopic" experience of living. This is advantageous for the benefits which follow directly in an enriched practical experience. The conclusions, or "objects," enrich gross experience by amplifying and enforcing the range of significance of the details of experience, by establishing known relations between apparently isolated items so that the larger significance is felt in every instance. Also they pave the way for the more effectual operation of intelligence and open the prospect of advance in fortune and welfare through intellectual activity.

Such benefits accruing from the use of an empirical approach would seem to be potential without reduction in the application of philosophical reflection upon religious affairs. In empiricism, knowledge objects are *as experienced*. This is to say they are "operational" in character, being construed from the point of view of a human being living by manipulating his environment. The form of such an outlook, while doubtless indigenous in American experience and congenial to the American temper, is sufficiently different from that which prevailed intellectually during the first one and a half millennia of Christianity to account for the sense of strangeness, of unsuitability, which is felt when the attempt is made to think the Christian evangel in terms of American empiricism. Yet such incongruity may well be grounded in the contrast existing between the cultural media rather than in any inherent contradiction.

Whatever may be held as opinion to the contrary notwithstanding, American pragmatic thinking does not preclude religious problems from consideration. Empirical thought definitely recognizes qualitative phenomena, among which the manifestations of religious experience occur. Dewey has made it plain that he not only would hold that all aspects of human experience as they actually occur are proper subject matter for deliberate reflection, but, because of the practical benefits potential in the use of empirical method in handling problems of men, he maintains that the extension of its use into the domain of higher human values is urgently imperative.

In the generation after World War I Dewey wrote:

Operational thinking needs to be applied to the judgment of values just as it has now finally been applied in conceptions of physical objects. Experimental empiricism in the field of ideas of good and bad is demanded to meet the conditions of the present situation.[7]

Recently, after World War II, he has repeated his plea.

Philosophy still has a work to do . . . . There is no phase of

life, educational, economic, political, religious, in which inquiry may not aid in bringing to birth that world which Matthew Arnold rightly said was as yet unborn. Present-day philosophy cannot desire a better work than to engage in the act of midwifery that was assigned to it by Socrates twenty-five hundred years ago.[8]

There seems no room for doubt that in the fundamental empiricism which grounds his philosophical reflections, Dewey would hold that whatever the operation of intelligence is, it is as fully that in religious experience as in any other mode of human affairs.

NATURAL

The one aspect of all empirical data which Dewey especially takes into account as he grapples with the problem of understanding and which has special significance for the problem of this discussion is particularly set forth in his view of nature. For him, nature does not designate some segment of experience within which a certain kind of object exists but denotes the general character of all experienced matter, in which the determinative trait is the interconnectedness of all events. Thus the nature of anything may be understood through a discovery of the manner in which it interacts with other things.

Such relations of nature extend far beyond actual experience and render existential events "capable of an infinite number of meanings" both in genetic significance—

The visible is set in the invisible; and in the end what is unseen decides what happens in the seen; the tangible rests precariously upon the untouched and ungrasped. The contrast and the potential maladjustment of the immediate, the conspicuous and focal phase of things, with those indirect and hidden factors which determine the origin and career of what is present, are indestructible features of any and every experience.[9]

and in ideal possibilities—

Nature thus supplies potential material for embodiment of ideals. Nature, if I may use the locution, is idealizable. It lends itself to operations by which it is perfected. The process is not a passive one. Rather nature gives, not always freely but in response to search, means and material by which the values we judge to have supreme quality may be embodied in existence.[10]

Nature and society include within themselves projections of ideal possibilities and contain the operations by which they are actualized . . . . But nature, including humanity, with all its defects and imperfections, may evoke heartfelt piety as the source of ideals, of possibilities, of aspirations in their behalf, and as the eventual abode of all attained goods and excellencies.[11]

Such a range of perspective is sufficiently copious to bring the phenomena of the religious aspect of experience within the realm of the natural, as Dewey conceives nature. Much of the traditional import of the supernatural, as defined in a dualistic frame of reference in which mind and matter were distinctively separated, is absorbed rather than denied in Dewey's conception of the natural.

That to which both mind and matter belong is the complex of events that constitute nature.[12]

In the traditional usage of the terms the "supernatural" was construed as the supramechanical, the supraphysical, the supramaterial, when "nature" was confined to these traits of existence. But with the reorientation of this term in Dewey's view of the universe, "nature" includes the "spiritual," the "ideal," the "invisible" characters, once associated only with the "supernatural." Nothing that is

related is conceded any existence *outside* nature. It remains to be established that, and how, specific beliefs in religion are related in the experience of men. In so far as they *are* related they cannot be "supernatural" from Dewey's point of view, however much they may be unique, spontaneous, original, different in their manifestations. Doubtless some will yet claim that religious objects are of a distinct sort in some unrelated realm apprehended only through mystic experience, but the historical data which constitute the factual content of the Christian proclamation and the empirical facts attested to in Christian history and biography serve to bring all this within the scope of Dewey's "nature." This is not to insinuate that Dewey himself is or is not impressed with this particular Christian interpretation of the data but simply to point out that the empirical character of the material definitely instates it within the purview of Dewey's thought. As much as any thinker may deny every historic or individual interpretation of that material it remains proper subject matter for reflection and for research. Since it is empirical it is natural, being interconnected with affairs of ordinary human experience. And because it is natural it will be seen to include the operation of intelligence.

The fact that religious conceptions have often placed major emphasis upon final causes while Dewey's conception omits final causes does not point to any necessary impasse in taking religious phenomena to be natural in Dewey's sense of the term. Dewey has noted:

The net result of the new scientific method was conception of nature as a mathematical-mechanical object. If modern philosophy, reflecting the tendencies of the new science, abolished final causes from nature, it was because concern with qualitative ends, already existing objects of possession and enjoyment, blocked inquiry, discovery and control, and ended in barren dialectical disputes about definitions and classifications."[13]

This is doubtless authentic history, and a valid cultural observation, but is obviously not to be taken as the basis for affirming a denial of final causes. It is just what it was phrased to be, an explanation of a trend of development in philosophical interest, and can serve as an item for consideration in appraising the instrumental nature of philosophy, but not as indicating the meaning of nature. The fact that Dewey has labored to expose the philosophical inadequacy of classic and traditional conceptions of nature as being substantival does not warrant the insinuation of a rival substantival view. Dewey has described nature as the character of events as experienced. This points to the present nature of nature, but does not even claim to define nature in any final or ultimate sense whatever.

The significance of such a conception of nature in the understanding and deliberate promotion of religious experience is even more sharply felt when the direct connection between the immediate and the sequential is recognized. Events as they occur are related in serial sequence; but they are also immediately had in enjoyment and suffering, in conscious awareness, wherein they both acquire worth and are perceived in their sequential histories.

What is more precisely pertinent to our present theme, the terminal outcome when anticipated (as it is when a moving cause of affairs is perceived) becomes an end-in-view, an aim, purpose, a prediction usuable as a plan in shaping the course of events."[14]

Since "by the nature of the case the occurrence of the immediate is at the mercy of the sequential order," and "objects of desire" can be perceived in their eventual his-

tories wherein are manifested the mechanisms by which their occurrence may be regulated,

reflection is concerned with the order which conditions, prevents and secures their occurrence,[15]

and so "matter" becomes the means for control in the manipulation of inaccessible, "ineffable," values. Within the scope of this insight every conceivable problem of education in religion is seen to be entirely within the range of intellection and deliberate control in the operation of experimental intelligence.

Much of the significance of this whole aspect of nature for the purpose of this discussion is set forth in the following passage from *Experience and Nature*.

"Effects," since they mark the release of potentialities, are more adequate indications of the nature of nature than are just "causes." Control of the occurrence of the complex depends upon its analysis into the more elementary; the dependence of life, sentiency and mind upon "matter" is thus practical or instrumental Lesser, more external fields of interaction are more manageable than are wider and more intimate ones, and only through managing the former can we direct the occurrence of the latter. Thus it is in virtue of the character of events which is termed matter that psycho-physical and intellectual affairs can be differentially determined. Every discovery of concrete dependence of life and mind upon physical events is therefore an addition to our resources. If life had mind and no mechanism, education, deliberate modification, rectification, prevention and constructive control would be impossible.[16]

In so far as religion is a "psychophysical and intellectual affair," whatever values inhere in the religious aspect of experience are also involved in experience with material physical elements. It is this natural aspect which establishes the function of intelligence as actually potential in affairs of religion and thus points to the possibility of manipulation and control.

HUMAN

Consideration of the nature of man as set forth in the philosophy of John Dewey is planned for extensive treatment in Chapter IV, but it is pertinent to this presentation of the operation of intelligence to note the place of man in nature. Man is taken, by Dewey, to be a special kind of natural event. Nature is manifested in man and actually disclosed in the activities and achievements of man. In fact there are times when the expression of Dewey's thought seems to suggest that nature is the primary factor, as when he writes:

The striving of man for objects of imagination is a continuation of natural processes; it is something man has learned from the world in which he occurs, not something which he arbitrarily injects into that world. When he adds perception and ideas to these endeavors, it is not after all he who adds; the addition is again the doing of nature and a further complication of its own domain.[17]

But even in this context he distinguishes the human as a special manifestation of nature. He goes on to say:

To act, to enjoy and suffer in consequence of action, to reflect, to discriminate and make differences in what had been but gross and homogeneous good and evil, according to what inquiry reveals of causes and effects; to act upon what is learned, to engage in new goods and evils is human, the course which manifests the course of nature.[18]

So while he obviously recognizes the unique character of the human, he nonetheless vigorously contends that whatever is human comes within the domain of the natural.

Much more important than the distinctive character of man is the significance in the total course of nature of that

manifestation which occurs in the processes of the conscious, purposeful acts of human beings. In consciousness
the relations found in nature as cause and effect are transformed into means and consequences, becoming susceptible
to direction.

When an interaction intervenes which directs the course of
change, the scene of natural interaction has a new quality and
dimension. This added type of interaction *is* intelligence. The
intelligent activity of man is not something brought to bear upon
nature from without, it is nature realizing its own potentialities,
in behalf of a fuller and richer issue of events.[19]

Since human activity is seen as natural process functioning
to modify existence, it would seem that self-consciousness
is thus a matter of great practical significance, involving the
alteration, the reconstruction, or even the regeneration of
the self. Obviously, this amounts to recognizing that with
the emergence of conscious human existence nature in man
begins to control consciously the further course of its own
development. Such deliberate redirection involves the abstractions which comprise human consciousness. Dewey
observes:

Until some acts and their consequences are discriminatingly
referred to the human organism and other energies and effects
are referred to other bodies, there is no leverage, no purchase,
with which to regulate the course of experience. The abstraction of certain qualities of things as due to human acts and
states is the *pou sto* of ability in control.[20]

Apparently such abstraction and manipulation in consciousness is not merely a possibility. It is actually a necessity for
certain results—

It is no mere play on words to say that the recognition of
psychological abilities is a necessary factor in subjecting the
energies of nature to use as instrumentalities for ends.[21]

It is pertinent to the problem of this discussion to note that Dewey holds the whole sweep of human experience, including all aspects of culture in whatever form, to be entirely and fully natural.

In experience, human relations, institutions, and traditions are as much a part of the nature in which and by which we live as is the physical world. Nature in this meaning is not "outside." [23]

This is not to say that all nature is in the human manifestation, but it is to say that all human is within the natural. In so far as intelligence will be seen as a natural process, all variations of human experience including thinking will be considered as intelligible. At the same time the importance of what takes place in man accrues from the unlimited relationships permeating all that is: when man is changed the world is changed. And since self-consciousness involves the potentiality of deliberate reformation of the self, it follows that the experience of man in self-consciousness is significant for the course of the world's affairs. There is seen here the principle of deliberate self-control, self-direction, manipulation, and reconstruction of actual events in terms of the interests and purposes of the self.

EXPERIENCE

The course of experience provides the structure within which experimental intelligence operates. Basically, experience is held to be simply "things interacting in certain ways," but the situation is characteristically described in terms of the biological aspect of an organism living through interaction with its environment. Despite this specific intellectual orientation, experience is not to be conceived as limited to physical or physiological levels of being.

Just as physical life cannot exist without the support of a physical environment, so moral life cannot go on without the support of a moral environment.[33]

It belongs to Dewey's conception of the homogeneity pervading all events to hold that an examination of the obvious (in this case the biological) will reveal the structure which exists in the obscure (e.g., the psychological). Thus the insights which Dewey has noted are to be taken as valid in any phase of consideration of human affairs.

Such interaction (experience) involves the welfare and fortunes of the living things, and thereby actually affects the world at large.

In an experience, things and events belonging to the world, physical and social, are transformed through the human context they enter, while the live creature is changed and developed through its intercourse with things previously external to it.[34]

The creative potentiality implied here gives both possibility and significance to the work of education.

Indeed, the business of education might be defined as an emancipation and enlargement of experience.[35]

This bears eventually upon the underlying thesis of this whole discussion, but it is sufficient here to recognize that experience provides the possibility of original, regenerative, and revolutionary effects in individual and social history as consequences in human affairs.

This possibility not only extends to any sort of effect in the career of an individual but it encompasses the occurrence of the individual himself. Dewey makes a special point of the occurrence of unique experiences.

For life is no uniform uninterrupted march or flow. It is a thing of histories, each with its own plot, its own inception and movement toward its close, each having its own particular rhythmic movement; each with its own unrepeated quality pervading it throughout."

Continuity throughout experience, both in expansion and duration, is emphasized as basically natural, yet the singular feature of the unique aspect is definitely recognized.

An experience has a unity that gives it its name, *that* meal, that storm, that rupture of friendship. The existence of this unity is constituted by a single *quality* that pervades the entire experience in spite of the variation of its contitutent parts."

What this insight implies can be felt in even more pronounced fashion when it is recalled that because "there is a unity of experience that can be expressed only as an experience," the basis exists for identity; which is to say, putting it more baldly, plurality of individuals is natural. There can be things, persons, in fact any sort of entities distinguishable as units at a certain level of experience. Later in this discussion the "self" will be more particularly examined, but this preliminary observation of its occurrence in experience as an altogether natural event will serve to place the most profound religious values within the range of the operation of intelligence, insomuch as that is a natural process.

Despite their unique characters such events as "selves" can be recognized, observed, and understood since they do have common structures:

The outline of the common pattern is set by the fact that every experience is the result of interaction between a live creature and some aspect of the world in which he lives."

Dewey specifically extends this concept in the secondary environment of ideas that it may be seen as a principle of experience throughout the whole range of relations:

The creature operating may be a thinker in his study and the environment with which he interacts may consist of ideas in-

stead of a stone. But the interaction of the two constitutes the total experience that is had, and the close which completes it is the institution of a felt harmony.[29]

Here is to be seen the inception of "self-consciousness": the phenomenon of nature experiencing itself in the total life history of an individual as an experience:

Experience, a serial course of affairs, with their own characteristic properties and relationships, occurs, happens, and is what it is. Among and within occurrences, not outside them, nor underlying them, are those events which are denominated selves.[30]

Unique experiences should not be thought of as occurring momentarily in isolated discrete fashion because it is said they are distinct affairs. Actually it is the continuity of experience persisting throughout nature which invests such experiences with meaning through additive cumulation in the natural process. With brilliant insight Dewey discovers here the source of human individuation.

But the process of living is continuous; it possesses continuity because it is an everlastingly renewed process of acting upon the environment and being acted upon by it, together with institution of relations between what is done and what is undergone. Hence experience is necessarily cumulative and its subject matter gains expressiveness because of cumulative continuity. The world we have experienced becomes an integral part of the self that acts and is acted upon in further experiences. In their physical occurrence, things and events experienced pass on and are gone. But something of their meaning and value is retained as an integral part of the self. Through habits formed in intercourse with the world, we also inhabit the world. It becomes a home and the home is part of our every experience.[31]

In other contexts Dewey has expanded this observation to indicate the source of all meaning is "prior experience," not merely of the one individual, but of any number who share and communicate their findings, and thus have an ideational experience of the whole connected series of events before such actually occur.

The beginning not only *is* the initial term in a *series* (as distinct from a *succession*), but it gains the *meaning* of subsequent activity moving toward a consequence of which it is the first member.[32]

The seeming chronological anomaly between this quotation and the one preceding disappears when it is kept in mind that the significance of the serial consequence leading from the first term to the last must be *experienced prior* to the first term being actualized, if the first term is to have the *meaning* which the consequence imparts. Through "self-consciousness" there must be experience of the whole future history to the very ultimate term in some fashion *before,* in order that the actual experience in history can be fully meaningful. Thus being conscious at any given instant of eventual destiny enhances the present moment far beyond what values accrue from an awareness of the immediate sensory situations, and from memories of past history.

The vast implications of this principle bring the whole future to bear upon the present moment.

But when an event has meaning, its potential consequence becomes its integral and funded feature. When the potential consequences are important and repeated, they form the very nature and essence of a thing, its defining, identifying and distinguishing form. To recognize the thing is to grasp its definition.[33]

For Dewey this occurs because the process of intellection has its genesis in the recognition of the direct relation between the former and the latter events in actual sequence.

All knowing and effort to know starts from some belief, some received and asserted meaning which is a deposit of prior experience, personal and communal.[34]

There is indicated here the wide import of social heritage

through this cumulative process since "experiences expressed are what they are because of experiences of the living and the dead that have shaped them." Certainly the accusation that Dewey fails to recognize the significance of the past in his interpretation of experience must be denied in the light of such an affirmation:

I do not for a moment suppose that the experiences of the past, personal and social, are of no importance. For without them we should not be able to frame any ideas whatever of the conditions under which objects are enjoyed nor any estimate of the consequences of esteeming and liking them. But past experiences are significant in giving us intellectual instrumentalities of judging just these points. They are tools, not finalities.[35]

This brief sketch of the structure of experience will be found ample to provide an adequate description of religious experience within the perspective of experimentalism. Any individual unique in his own identity can conceive of himself as an experience which can transcend that of which he is immediately aware. Also he can experience ideas in his intellectual environment which are significant in their funded meanings because of the experiences of others, who have expressly shared their findings through social processes.

It now remains to be seen that in all this, intelligence is involved. This is plainly so stated by Dewey:

The organism is a part of the natural world; its interactions with it are genuine additive phenomena. When with the development of symbols, also a natural occurence, these interactions are directed towards anticipated consequences, they gain the quality of intelligence, and knowledge accrues.[36]

With this possibility of knowledge is included the possibility of direction of activity, and this leads directly to noting that the function of thinking is intrinsic in the human process.

In other words, all experienced objects have a double status. They are individualized, consummatory, whether in the way of enjoyment or of suffering. They are also involved in a continuity of interactions and changes, and hence are causes and potential means of later experiences. Because of this dual capacity, they become problematic.[37]

Something of the practical import of intellectualization in reflection upon this whole aspect of affairs can be recognized when it is realized that to understand the course of experience in which an individual becomes conscious of himself as a person and as a potential factor in the affairs of the world, is to prepare the way for self-disposition and self-direction.

For a perceived mode of becoming is always ready to be translated into a method of production and direction.[38]

The close relevance of this insight to the general problems of the manipulation of religious experience will be duly noted later in this discussion.

THINKING

The nature of the thinking process has received extensive analysis and elaboration in the works of John Dewey, but in this discussion attention will be focused upon the practical significance of this operation especially in the matter of directing the course of affairs. Thinking has been defined as a process that originates in problematic situations where perplexity is experienced because of dubious possibilities or conflicting interests. Although description of reflective thinking is usually couched in bio-social terms, representing a living organism in interaction with environment, the occurrence of thinking is looked for in human experience. The human being is conceived of as possessing unique capacity to experience any number of various potential

meanings in any given situation, while inhibiting overt response. Such mental activity is seen to be deliberately directed and extended by experimenting imaginatively with different ideas in the situation in hand. This is the procedure called "thinking," and is so to be understood as an active process of investigation by the use of operational ideas, in the search for the best possible solution of the problem confronting the organism (the man). However, such exploratory research by way of mental processes is by no means innocent. The course of the investigation entails definite results.

Vital inference always leaves one who thinks with a world that is experienced as different in some respect, for some object in it has gained in clarity and orderly arrangement. Genuine thinking winds up, in short, with an appreciation of new values.[39]

Since thinking is a mode of experiencing, it is to be understood that something is happening while thinking is going on. For Dewey, thinking is a particular type of organic response: a response guided by a plan or an idea of what will happen if certain things are done. Thus, thinking is not followed by action; it rather requires action in order to complete itself. Changes are occurring. It is probable that a close criticism of this idea would confine such changes primarily within the situation in which the man is involved. Yet in so far as he is part of the world and through the means of communication may share his own findings with any number of other persons to a limitless extent, thus far the world is different because he thought. Certainly change has been initiated and directed through his thinking. Dewey guards this idea from any easy perversion into subjectivism by noting:

If we define "mental" through exclusion of overt acts that terminate in a changed environment, nothing merely mental can actually resolve doubt or clarify conclusion.[40]

And again when he writes:

Action is the means by which a problematic situation is resolved.[41]

The changes which are brought about through thinking
are directly caused by the introduction of something new
from outside the specific situation into the consideration
of the problem. It is this function which the mind of man
is competent to perform. Herein lie inestimable possibilities.
This phase of the knowledge process is thus described:

All reflective inquiry starts from a problematic situation, and no
such situation can be settled in its own terms. It evolves into
a resolved situation only by means of introduction of material
not found in the situation itself.[42]

It is worthy of note that such "new" material may be an
instrumentality of intellectual procedure, a method to be
added to other methods, to produce an original novel construction that may be especially suited to handle the issue
involved.

An essence which is a method of procedure can be linked to
other methods of procedure so as to yield new methods; to bring
about a revision of old methods, and form a systematic and
ordered whole—all without reference to any application of any
method to any particular set of concrete abstractions from any
particular consequences which the methods or logical universals
are to regulate.[43]

Such an observation will help to keep the operation of
thinking from being limited within the physical problems
suggested in the biological orientation of the descriptions
given.

Thinking functions throughout conscious experience according to the problems faced by men, and so this process
is to be looked for wherever human interests are involved.

Its importance seems to be indicated in the scope of this remark:

In short, the thing actually at stake in any serious deliberation is not a difference of quantity, but what kind of person is one to become, what sort of self is in the making, what kind of a world is making."

Not only are such changes possible in the immediate situation to an indefinite degree but the results of thinking are again available to innumerable other persons through communication. And so by virtue of the cumulative character of experience noted above benefits accrue indefinitely for subsequent generations of society.

The great reward of exercising the power of thinking is that there are no limits to the possibility of carrying over into the objects and events of life, meanings originally acquired by thoughtful examination, and hence no limit to the continual growth of meaning in human life. A child of today may see meanings in things that were hidden from Ptolemy and Copernicus because of the results of reflective investigations that have occurred in the meantime."

Thus an ascending spiral of advance through human activity in thinking would seem to augment the cultural heritage of any group in its history. In the field of contemporary religious thought an interesting sidelight from this idea is thrown upon the tactics of both those who would return directly to apostolic times for authoritative norms of faith and practice, and those who would seek to evaluate the authenticity of Christian sources by direct historical criticism. The former are commonly held to be of the ultraconservative type, the latter of the ultraliberal type. It would seem that both stand to lose significant benefits funded in nineteen centuries of Christian experience by failing to take for their basic ideas the data of Christian faith as it is now held in the historic formulations. This procedure on their part may account for the dubious authenticity of either approach. Certainly the thinking of generations of mankind as naturally embodied in the culture of any group has potentiality for guidance of contemporary thought.

Examination of the past may be the chief and decisive factor in thought.[46]

It is in this creative aspect of thinking, whereby novel results in the world of affairs are obtained, that the natural possibility of directing conduct is to be seen.

Knowing is itself a mode of practical action and is *the* way of interaction by which other natural interactions become subject to direction.[47]

Thinking itself is carried on under direction,

Inquiry proceeds by reflection, by thinking; but *not*, most decidedly, by thinking as conceived in the older tradition, as something cooped up within "mind." For experimental inquiry or thinking signifies *directed activity*, doing something which varies the conditions under which objects are observed and directly had by instituting new arrangements among them.[48]

And thus through thinking direction is given to overt action. This idea is reflected in the following quotations which point the possibility and the potentiality of directive thought:

Only when things about us have meaning for us, only when they signify consequences that can be reached by using them in certain ways, is any such thing as intentional, deliberate control of them possible.[49]

Ideas that are plans of operations to be performed are integral factors in actions which change the face of the world.[50]

Such direction may be funded for unlimited future use in knowledge objects.

For the outcome of experienced objects which are begotten by operations which define thinking, take into themselves, as part of their own funded and incorporated meaning, the relation to other things disclosed by thinking.[51]

It is because such "experience objects" can be expressed symbolically in written language that literature is directly a means of enlarging and improving the mind. Despite their apparently abstruse character, abstractions as expressed and communicated in language have unique instrumental value.

Thus the most technical philosophical works are potentially significant for practical affairs, and even the theoretical interpretations of religious beliefs will have practical significance "within limits of probability."

Certainly it follows that all thinking is ground for the exercise of intelligence, which is the deliberate direction of action on the basis of operational knowledge of the consequences to be expected. The great emphasis upon thinking (as a problem solving operation) in modern education is thus seen to be sound; and the aim of the modern curriculum to lead the child to experience the subject matter in hand is a practical recognition that "thinking arises out of a directly experienced situation."[52] Dewey was probably referring to education in general when he wrote:

It is evident that education is primarily concerned with thinking as it actually takes place in individual human beings.[53]

But he was undoubtedly pointing toward an educational program based upon the practical potentialities in the instrumental function of thinking when he said:

Probably the most frequent cause of failure in school to secure genuine thinking from students is the failure to insure the existence of an experienced situation of such a nature as to call out thinking in the way in which these out-of-school situations do.[54]

This seems to be the insight needed to understand the sterility of much education in morals and in religion. When the educational procedure fails to lead the pupil into an actual participation in religious experience so that "thinking" is called for, and decision, choice, commitment is definitely challenged and actually made, the pupil may spend ever so much time and mental energy in "learning about," but he will never actually learn what belongs to religious experience in the terms of those who actually know. Certainly there has been no operation of intelligence, as we shall now recognize this factor in living.

INTELLIGENCE

"The constructively instrumental office of intelligence" occurs in the course of conduct as "a quality of some acts," particularly in the aspect of directive manipulation.

"Thought," reason, intelligence, whatever word we wish to use, is existentially an adjective (or better an adverb) not a noun. It is disposition of activity, a quality of that conduct which foresees consequences of existing events, and which uses what is foreseen as a plan and method of administering affairs.[55]

Thus it may be conceived as a distinctive "way" some events manifest in their occurrence. The concept can be more definitely marked when attention is focused upon changes in the course of interaction.

When an interaction intervenes which directs the course of change, the scene of natural interaction has a new quality and dimension. This added type of interaction *is* intelligence.[56]

The operation of intelligence is noted "in the modification of conditions, including all the guidance that is given by means of ideas, both direct and symbolic." Despite the fact that such ideas are held to occur only in the mind of man,

intelligence is taken by Dewey primarily as it appears in the course of natural events, rather than as some factor genetically human. Apparently Dewey is careful to contain intelligence in the altogether natural, thus guarding against any possibility of conceiving "intelligence" as being an element of extranatural origin or character. In fact, Dewey goes so far as to say:

Intelligence becomes ours in the degree in which we use it and accept responsibility for consequences. It is not ours originally or by production. "*It* thinks" is a truer psychological statement than "*I* think."[57]

The full significance of this pointed emphasis is not too clear. The obvious accent upon the natural origin of this quality of events seems almost redundant in view of the known perspective maintained in Dewey's thinking, which takes man as an event in nature and of nature. The question arises whether any "thinking" ever occurs in "it" before "I" exist. What Dewey has in mind is probably well understood when it is remembered that for him the environment is seen as playing an active role in suggesting possible modes of response. These suggestions are also grounded in the culturally conditioned experience of the individual. Thus the subject, the ego, the "I" is not a private psychical substance for Dewey. It is probable that Dewey was guarding here against misunderstanding of his view, in the light of philosophical ideas commonly held in his time but which he held to be unacceptable. Thus he points out:

A man is intelligent not in virtue of having reason which grasps first and indemonstrable truths about fixed principles, in order to reason deductively from them to the particulars which they govern, but in virtue of his capacity to estimate the possibilities of a situation and to act in accordance with his estimate.[58]

Here it seems more apparent that Dewey is concerned to hold "intelligence" as an entirely natural process for the

sake of understanding its operation. There is to be nothing
occult or supernatural in it. By the same sign he has
rendered a service in emphasizing that the operation of intelligence, the actual occurrence of this supervisory delib-
erative reflection upon and direction of events involving the
conscious participation of man, can be controlled. In other
words, man can be intelligent in the exercise of his intelligence. In fact, man's interest in his own unique nature
conceived in view of his eventual destiny is not to be seen
as an artificial imposition of some energetic religionism or
moralism. It is to be recognized for what it is. It is nature
manifesting its own potentialities at the higher levels of
experience.

Intelligence occurs only after activity has already begun.

Impulse is primary and intelligence is secondary and in some
sense derivative. There should be no blinking of this fact. But
recognition of it as a fact exalts intelligence. For thought is not
the slave of impulse to do its bidding . . . . What intelligence
has to do in the service of impulse is to act not as its obedient
servant but as its clarifier and liberator . . . . Intelligence converts desire into plans, systematic plans based on assembling
facts, reporting events as they happen, keeping tab on them and
analyzing them.[59]

By virtue of this very function of appraisal, selection, and
revision, intelligence interferes with the automatic movement of natural processes. It introduces an element of self-
control and self-direction, and thus becomes "the key to
freedom." The genesis of this operation seems to be a
matter of seeing "relations."

The action and its consequence must be joined in perception.
This relationship is what gives meanings; to grasp it is the
objective of all intelligence.[60]

As the operation proceeds, "meaning" is enhanced as the
"consequences" are noted. Thus, though secondary in emer-

gence, it is basically determinative in function, and in that very aspect it is enriching and enlarging in its effect upon human affairs.

When examined more closely, it will be seen that the function of guiding control develops with "recognition of a method of procedure, and of the alliance of insight into method with possibility of control." Such technique is to be discovered in "ordinary organic environmental adjustments," and becomes capable of extension into a "larger and larger field of ideas." Just as intelligence itself, while noted as a secondary manifestation in experience, is more important than primary impulse, so is the operation of intelligence in the area of "ideas" more important than, even though derived from, its manifestation in external affairs. Dewey says:

In matters predominantly physical we know that all control depends upon conscious perception of relations obtaining between things, otherwise one cannot be used to affect the other . . . . Clearly we have not carried the plane of conscious control, the direction of action by perception of connections, far enough . . . just where connections and interdependences are most numerous, intimate and pervasive, in living, psychophysical activity, we most ignore unity and connection, and trust most unreservedly in our deliberate beliefs to the isolated and specific, which signifies that in action we commit ourselves to the unconscious and sub-conscious, to blind instinct and impulse and routine, disguised and rationalized by all sorts of honorific titles.[61]

That such dereliction is fundamentally perilous throughout the whole range of human experience is expressed in this pronouncement:

As long as our own fundamental psychophysical attitudes in dealing with external things are subconscious, our conscious attention given only to the relations of external things, so long will our perception of the external situations be subject at its root to perversion . . . .[62]

It would be difficult to conceive more far-reaching significance of the operation of intelligence in personal affairs or state more urgently the imperative importance of its diligent exercise.

The origin of the operation of intelligence is grounded in the normal course of affairs. Natural events have "endings," "termini," commonly to be taken as "effects." When nature becomes aware of itself in consciousness so that the course of an event as it could move on to its completion is recognized, such foresight makes possible the transforming of "ends" into "ends-in-view," as "when a particular consequence is foreseen, and being foreseen is consciously adopted by desire and deliberately made the directive purpose of action." When the course of an event is so construed that only one ending seems possible, conscious adoption of the "end" as the "end-in-view" will be so significant that the "means" may come to be esteemed as important as the "consequences" they are taken to produce. Actually such estimation is directly grounded in an appreciation of the consequence that will follow. Dewey has observed:

Willingness to work for ends by means of acts not naturally attractive is best attained by securing an appreciation of the value of the end, that a sense of its value is transferred to its means of accomplishment.[63]

The "end-in-view" as the object of thought is appraised as being important and valid through the exercise of experimental inquiry, wherein "the validity of the object of thought depends upon the *consequences* of the operations which define the object of thought."

The test of ideas, of thinking generally, is found in the consequence of the acts to which the ideas lead, that is in the new arrangements of things which are brought into existence.[64]

It is this validating function of intelligence that seems to distinguish intelligence itself as the greatest value in nature. At the same time the developing of capacity and skill in the exercise of intelligence is to be seen as the most important task in education, inasmuch as the direction of the total activities of the individual is obviously the most significant factor in all that pertains to fortune and welfare.

The intrinsic bent in the operation of intelligence is toward the future. Any attempt to know the present or to appraise its meaning in experimental terms focuses attention at once upon what will occur in consequence of this present event. Dewey has pointed out that such interest in the future is primarily related to the problem of the present.

After all, the object of foresight of consequences is not to predict the future. It is to ascertain the meaning of present activities and to secure, as far as possible, a present activity with a unified meaning . . . . Our concern is with the significance of that slight fraction of total activity which starts from ourselves.[65]

Since "thought about future happenings is the only way we can judge the present," it would seem to follow obviously that

Dominating *intellectual* preoccupation with the future is the way by which efficiency in dealing with the present is attained.[66]

Throughout his whole examination of this aspect of the operation of intelligence Dewey does not relax his primary interest in the immediate practical issue of living in the most successful fashion now. He states it plainly:

Intelligence is concerned with foreseeing the future so that action may have order and direction.[67]

It is not then a matter of whim nor of curiosity, nor any craven withdrawal from the practical present situation, which prompts interest in the future. The very nature of affairs as they take place in time determines that there will be a forward cast to all intellectual activity that is concerned at all with human fortune.

It may be noted further that such intelligent manipulation of the present in the light of what is judged about the future actually affects the eventual future as it will occur. Thus, forseeing the future and appraising the present in terms of the future actually has bearing upon the course of events as they will develop. Dewey points out:

Intelligent action is not concerned with the bare consequences of the thing known, but with consequences *to be* brought into existence by action conditioned on the knowledge.[68]

Despite this interest in the sort of future which will follow present acts, the primary bearing of the operation of intelligence is upon the actual immediate present. It is most important to recognize this.

Control of future living, such as it may turn out to be, is wholly dependent upon taking his present activity, seriously and devotedly, as an end, not a means. And a man has his hands full in doing well what now needs to be done. Until men have formed the habit of using intelligence fully as a guide to present action they will never find out how much control of future contingencies is possible.[69]

In all this the burden of eventual outcome rests in the handling of the present in its immediate terms in the light of an understanding of its future bearings. The prospect of a deliberately constructed future is dependent upon an intelligent disposition of the issues of the present. The implication of this ambivalent significance is that this aspect of the operation of intelligence seems to lead directly into an area of possibilities commonly recognized as being in the field of religious experience.

Knowledge . . . puts in our possession the instrumentality by means of which preference may be an intelligent or intentional factor in constructing a future by wary and prepared action.

Knowledge of special conditions and relations is instrumental to the action which is in turn an instrument of production of situations having qualities of added significance and order. To be capable of such action is to be free.[70]

Throughout this chapter the conception of intelligence as set forth in the philosophy of John Dewey has been presented in its original form, that a clear impression of its character might be had in mind. The subject matter of Dewey's philosophy includes all empirical data taken as it occurs for what it is worth without arbitrary distinction or preference. Such material is held to manifest the nature of nature, the total continuum of all events, and the complex of everything in indefinite relationship. Nature is marked by characteristic differences. Man is a unique manifestation of nature in which nature becomes aware of itself in part, even to having experience of experience. Experience is the interaction of the live creature in and with its world, in the course of which changes occur. Thinking is a special form of experience in which there is deliberate direction of change, in the course of which intelligence is manifested when nature moves to realize itself by guiding activity in the light of known consequence to be expected. Since nature empirically includes a religious aspect, the processes sketched in this chapter will be found actual in the field of religion.

Inasmuch as religious experience occurs in human affairs, it is important to note the distinctive traits of human nature, and to this the next chaper is assigned.

IV: THE NATURE OF MAN

The characterization of man as presented in the philosophy of John Dewey must be held within due perspective to be adequately understood. The demands of continuity in analysis, required to develop generalizations about the nature of man, tend to simplifications that could easily leave an erroneous impression about his view of the significance of human personality. It is not so simple to avoid the trend to a misleading reduction in the estimate of man when one reads the words of Justice Holmes, which Dewey quotes with seeming approval:

We do know that a certain complex of energies can wag its tail and another can make a syllogism.[1]

A careful examination of the context of these words will discover that no harm was meant, or perhaps done, to the character of man; yet they scarcely seem suited to serve for a complete designation of man as a basis for recognition of his potentialities to achieve personal, moral, and cultural values. Dewey's own words in writing about man are no less technical:

Yet if man is within nature, not a little god outside, and is within as a mode of energy inseparably connected with other modes, interaction is the one unescapable trait of every human concern; thinking, even philosophic thinking is not exempt. This interaction is subject to partiality because the human factor has bent and bias.[2]

The needed corrective here is a constant awareness of the abstract instrumental character of this approach, which should inhibit any final revaluation of the actual import

of man as a concrete person by criteria construed within this deliberately limited perspective. What follows in this presentation of the Nature of Man as set forth in Dewey's works will constitute a descriptive sketch pointing out significant aspects in which the operation of intelligence may be noted and observed. Whatever or whoever man is, as a form of nature, he manifests these traits, described here in experimentalist terms, throughout his experience, including the religious. By noting the operation of intelligence in these aspects of human experience, a basis will be established for an understanding of the function of intelligence in religious affairs.

MIND

As the human organism maintains its precarious existence in a hazardous world, its organic responses exhibit mental quality when overt action is inhibited to permit reflective inquiry into indeterminate and problematic situations so that eventual behavior may be intelligent. Consciousness is a state of awareness of the significance of objects: an awareness derived from the changes in feeling aroused by the objects. Communication of such awareness to other human beings involves the use of symbols which become signs of the meanings being shared. Thus language emerges as various forms of the art of discourse. In the course of this whole process mind is developed,

and so "mind" is an added property assumed by a feeling creature, when it reaches that organized interaction with other living creatures which is language, communication . . . . This state of things in which qualitatively different feelings are not just had, but are significant of objective difference, is mind. Feelings are no longer just felt. They have and they make *sense*; record and prophesy.[3]

In keeping with his general view of man, Dewey maintains that mind is entirely natural and manifests itself at the highest level of complex and intimate interaction between natural events.

Through the use of symbols man has unique capacity to manipulate meanings so as to direct natural events, and thus to regulate the course of affairs in some measure.

In the degree that responses take place to the doubtful *as* the doubtful, they acquire mental quality. If they are such as to have a directed tendency to change the precarious and problematic into the secure and resolved, they are *intellectual* as well as mental. Acts are then relatively more instrumental and less consummatory or final; even the latter are haunted by a sense of what may issue from them.[4]

Thus, fundamentally, "mind" is to be taken as having transitive significance, as when Dewey points out:

Mind is primarily a verb. It denotes all the ways in which we deal consciously and expressly with the situations in which we find ourselves.[5]

And yet, also, it has a structure, for mind "denotes the whole system of meanings as they are embodied in the workings of organic life." "Organic" here by no means implies any limitation to the physiological, but rather it is to be so understood that "'mind' denotes every mode and variety of interest in, and concern for, things: practical, intellectual, and emotional."

Thus the single term "mind," while it serves to denote a particular form of interaction, in which nature is seen as directing its own further course of action and experience, must be understood from at least two different points of view, displaying an ambivalence in meaning which will be noted again and again throughout all examination of human affairs. The individual and the social, though they do not

contradict each other, are sufficiently different in constitution and in perspective that they may appear in notable contrast. At the same time they are so definitely grounded in the one organismic experience that they can never be separated in existence or in operation. Yet they can be distinguished, and profitably so, when the aim is to understand the processes involved. The primary significance of "mind" for Dewey is that of function—where thinking is employed to achieve the better response in a situation—and this seems obviously to be a trait of the behavior of the individual. But the other, or social, aspect of "mind" is no less real for Dewey, and is perhaps even more significant within the outlook of education: namely, that "mind" is "the body of organized meanings by means of which events of the present have significance for us." This secondary significance of "mind" might be taken as direction in the course of human affairs, and seems just as basically to be social in nature.

Dewey emphasizes the social origin and nature of "mind" which develops as a child learns the structure of meanings shared by a human community.

But the whole history of science, art and morals proves that the mind that appears *in* individuals is not as such individual mind. The former is in itself a system of belief, recognitions and ignorance, of acceptances and rejections, of expectancies and appraisals of meanings which have been instituted under the influence of custom and tradition.[6]

While it is recognized that ideas occur only in the mentation process of individuals, it is held that their significance and meaning extend beyond the range of individual consciousness and somehow persist in an actual structure of meanings apart from and beyond any particular individual mind. In discussing the mechanism involved, Dewey writes:

There must be a story, some whole, an integrated series of episodes. This connected whole is mind, as it extends beyond a particular process of consciousness and conditions it. There must also be now-occurring events, to which meanings are assigned in terms of a story taking place. Episodes do not mean what they would mean if occurring in some different story. They have to be perceived in terms of the story, as its forwardings and fulfillings.[7]

The "story" itself (as "mind") "changes slowly through the joint tuition of interest and circumstance" as the repeated "events" occur in the variant affairs of different individuals. Dewey conceives mind as a development within the behavior of "a living organism that has to search for its food, that selects and rejects according to its present conditions and needs, and that retains only what it digests and transmutes into part of the energy of its own being." He holds that "an experienced, well informed mind" is capable of elaborating a fertile suggestion "until there results an idea that is quite different from the one with which the mind started." Not only do novel formulations of older ideas thus issue from mental activities, but some permanent change seems to follow.

As the growth of the body is through the assimilation of food, so the growth of the mind is through the logical organization of subject matter.[8]

This whole view of mind as a real structure of meanings, gradually changing because of the variant individual "episode" experiences, needs to be qualified by the realization that in so far as there is an intrinsic element of objective reality or history in the "story" of factors that have been given or of events that have been unalterably had, there will be perduring patterns in certain aspects of the "story." However, the understanding and perchance the evaluation of the "given" or the history will continue to be modified

according to the course of the actual experiences of those involved in it.

Thus it appears that "mind" in its structural aspect, as an organized system of meanings largely "social" in nature, is susceptible to modification because of the unique experiences of individuals who employ that mind in their own specific living. It now is to be noted that the "story," the total eventual continuum of meanings, which reaches beyond the area of consciousness, not only in the experience of this individual, but also beyond the bounds of his experience into the experiences of others, determines the formulation of ideas in the individual mind even more than may be realized at the time.

But we are capable of getting ideas from what is read because of an organized system of meanings of which we are not at any one time completely aware. Our mathematical or political "mind" is the system of such meanings as possess and determine our particular apprehensions or ideas.[8]

It is this reality that accounts for benefits accruing from counseling and conferring, when the individual's comprehension of his own problems is clarified and improved in the course of sharing his experience with another whose consciousness is freer from emotional disturbance, or whose perspective is better because of being more detached, and who can thus help the individual to interpret and to understand his problem. That is to say, putting it more baldly, the counselor through his acquaintances with the counselee, and in sympathetic rapport with him, having acquired a grasp of that person's mind, his "story," leads the counselee to an understanding of his immediate pressing problems by helping him to be aware of meanings which belong to him, to his "story," and by suggesting to him competent ideas to deal with this situation in terms of the counselee's own "mind."

Also, it is at this point that the importance of ideological propaganda can be glimpsed. It would appear that the effectual nurture of any individual mind with the basic tenets of a particular ideological system would deeply influence the future course of thinking of that person. That this would be as true in the case of the benign, as of the malignant in human affairs, grounds whatever hope there may be for the achieving of that which is good in the future of mankind, as a result of education.

The fact that various and sundry "minds" may be current in any social environment poses the problem of discrimination and choice in which the operation of intelligence is of crucial importance. Also the significance of education is herein indicated. While the spontaneous freedom of the individual may never be entirely prohibited, the predisposing import of the "mind" in which the individual has been developed, and to which he has been committed, is so great that it behooves all who care for the predominance of any system of ideas to seek to win and to train recruits who will in turn maintain and disseminate that "mind" to others. There are many different "stories": it is a matter of vital importance to ground others in that "story" which is deemed good for the welfare and happiness of mankind.

The empirical source of ideas indicates the bearing of past events upon mind, and through mind upon the management of present affairs. "The purport of past affairs is present in the momentary cross-sectional idea in a way which is more intimate, direct and pervasive than the way of recall." This is doubtless because the individual has actually been affected in the course of what he has endured. "Tendencies of observation, desire and emotion are shaped by prior experiences" so that as an "organism" he "carries

past experience in itself not by conscious memory but by direct charge."

The sub-conscious of a civilized adult reflects all the habits he has acquired; that is to say, all the organic modifications he has undergone.[10]

The profound significance of this insight for character education is obvious, even as it would seem to be unlimited in its scope.

New ideas come leisurely yet promptly to consciousness only when work has previously been done in forming the right doors by which they may gain entrance. Subconscious maturation precedes creative production in every line of human endeavor.[11]

These "right doors" are doubtless the practical results of actual events in the course of past affairs, and yet each present situation presents another actual problem sufficiently different and unique to challenge original handling as of now for which the only solution would seem to be a fresh approach in practical fashion.

If doubt and indeterminateness were wholly within the mind . . . whatever they may signify . . . purely mental processes ought to get rid of them. But experimental procedure signifies that actual alteration of an external situation is necessary to effect the conversion. A *situation* undergoes, through operations directed by thought, transition from the problematic to settled, from internal discontinuity to coherency and organization.[12]

Thus it is more accurate to speak of "altering the situation" than it is to refer to "changing one's mind." The fact that "mind" is thus concretely involved in actual affairs, together with the fact that in its function it determines the course of future events, makes all that happens in the mind of man a matter of grave practical importance.

The principle set forth in the preceding paragraph which stresses the primary importance of "altering the situation" as an essential part of "changing one's mind" is to be taken as applicable in intellectual matters as well as in practical affairs. The demonstration of a rational idea in the course of logical argument is actually an arranging of intellectual processes in the intellectual realm, and the conclusion as such is actually an objective affair involving the participation of the hearer of the argument. In just this way, the presentation of some religious belief to the attention of an individual challenging his personal acceptance of a projected relationship involving himself is actually more external and objective: it is "an arrangement of the situation" on the part of the preacher, the evangelist: the extent to which the hearer follows with personal committal is the extent to which he will be changed in himself.

From what has been noted it will be obvious that the process of inculcating the meanings of any particular "mind" in any individual will involve active participation in the resolving of problematic situations in which the individual is an integral factor. Such situations may be of the concrete physical sort, or they may be rational problems, intellectual dilemmas, to be solved in logical demonstration. Also they may be personal problems in which the issue is a matter of choosing the kind of person one wants to be, the kind of world one wants to have. Apparently the procedures of education aiming to ground and to culture any specific "mind" in any individual will involve encountering problematic situations involving the pupil and thus challenging determinative choice in the thinking thus generated. When once the individual settles upon a certain character for himself, the direction taken in the mental processes is practically determined. It seems to follow that directed participation in a controlled situation does actually result in a mind of designed pattern, and thus in a future course of conduct predetermined by the

direction implicit in that control. And so what happens in the religious experience of man can never be a matter of indifference to the interests of either the individual or society: the potentialities for good and for evil are too great and too real to be ignored. It is the importance of this fact that makes the exercise of intelligence in education, in religion, so practical and important. In so far as religious matters involve the mind of man, and certainly in the promotion of religious experience this is the case, there is opportunity for the operation of intelligence in its fullest scope. This will now be seen even more clearly when attention is focused upon the nature of the "self."

THE SELF

While the nature of man comprises the infinite relationships involving him as an integral part, the particularity of the biological organism grounds the occurrence of the individual whose own specific choices in the exercise of his mind will have definitive consequences in the ongo of affairs. Out of the welter of interaction, as a result of "the way the organism reacts and responds," an individual existence emerges as a matter of course. Dewey describes this event in terms that seem to suggest it should be taken almost as something "given":

At different times we brood over different things; we entertain purposes that, as far as consciousness is concerned, are independent, being each appropriate to its own occasion; we perform different acts, each with its own particular result. Yet as they all proceed from one living creature they are somehow bound together below the level of intention. They work together, and finally something is born almost in spite of conscious personality, and certainly not because of its deliberate will.[13]

It is impossible to escape the impression that Dewey has

touched here upon the very core of what is involved in
personality problems, as well as in religious values. The
nativity of this entity as indicated above challenges attention and interpretation, but the omission of further
elaboration by Dewey himself renders speculation dubious.
It is possible that its location in the subconscious is sufficient to warrant no further attempt at definition; and yet
its implications for the understanding of human personality would seem to justify further examination. It would
be quite alien to Dewey's thought to admit the existence of
anything unrelated to all else, and so it is probable that the
emergence of this "singularity," while obscure and perhaps
inscrutable, is certainly neither occult nor mysterious. It
is quite probable that what he had in mind here is just what
he described as follows in another context:

In conclusion, it may be asserted that "soul" when freed from all
traces of traditional materialistic animism denotes the qualities
of psycho-physical activities as far as these are organized into
unity. Some bodies have souls preeminently as some conspicu-
ously have fragrance, color and solidity. To make this statement
is to call attention to properties that characterize these bodies,
not to import a mysterious, non-natural entity or force.[14]

While every sympathy may be felt with Dewey's concern
here to avoid misunderstanding about the source of the
"soul" as being from within the body, it will also be well to
keep in mind that this is experimental description of functional properties. Dewey's caution to avoid complication
with metaphysical matters must not mislead the reader to
assume a denial of, or any manner of reference to, such
matters. It is important to hold the point exactly where
Dewey held it: that he was not intending any adoption of,
or reference to, or collusion with, other concepts indicated
by the word "soul." At the same time it would seem rather
obvious that his choice of this word does intend to mean

that he feels he is referring to that function in personality development which in the past had been designated "soul."

It is doubtless a tribute to Dewey's faithfulness to his principle of accepting empirical data as they are found that he should identify his conception in the common terminology of common speech. That his use of the word "soul" was no inadvertent slip of the pen but a deliberate pointing of his thought into the common intellectual structures of our culture is even more plainly indicated in the following passage:

When the organization called soul is free, moving and operative, initial as well as terminal, it is spirit. Qualities are both static, substantial, and transitive. Spirit quickens; it not only is alive, but spirit gives life. Animals are spirited, but man is a living spirit. He lives in his works, and his works do follow him. Soul is form, spirit informs. It is the moving function of that of which soul is the substance. Perhaps the words soul and spirit are so heavily laden with traditional mythology and sophisticated doctrine that they must be surrendered; it may be impossible to recover for them in science and philosophy the realities designated in idiomatic speech. But the realities are there, by whatever names they may be called.[15]

Without taking unfair advantage of the author of this passage, it would seem to be plain beyond doubt that Dewey held the historic terms as being indicative of actual conditions and events. Nothing more is needed to establish the fact that in Dewey's opinion the accepted language used in discourse about the phenomena of religious experience made sound reference to actual events. Experimental description and interpretation may proceed upon a more abstract and therefore a more intellectual plane, producing broader generalization and facilitating more efficient manipulation, but it does not cast aspersion upon the validity of the basic discriminations reported by the common sense of those who have reflected upon their own religious experiences.

Whatever may be the source of the unifying principle, and however the origin of the self may be understood, it seems clear that man as an event in this pluralistic universe does arrive at an awareness of himself as one; that he identifies his own career as the career of that one person he is; and that he conceives his highest values as involved in the existence and the fortunes of that one self he esteems himself to be. Dewey has summarized this general conclusion in these words:

That an individual, possessed of some mode and degree of organized unity, participates in the genesis of every experienced situation, whether it is an object or an activity, is evident. That the way in which it is engaged affects the quality of the situation experienced is evident. That the way in which it is engaged has consequences that modify not merely the environment but which react to modify the active agent; that every form of life in the higher organisms constantly conserves some consequences of its prior experiences, is also evident. The constancy and pervasiveness of the operative presence of the self as a determining factor in all situations is the chief reason why we give so little heed to it; it is more intimate and omnipresent in experience than the air we breathe.[16]

It would beggar the imagination to attempt to grasp the sweeping import of the truth revealed in this insight: certainly there is left no room for doubt that the self, the "soul," the "spirit," designate an aspect of existence that is significant above all else. When it is now recalled that this "self," this "individual," is not preexistent, nor is it unalterable; but that it is "being made," and that by processes that can be cognized and identified, the import of the achieving of selfhood attains religious proportions.

Dewey has pressed his analysis of the genesis of the

self to simple organic interactions. Thus he writes:

Whenever the activities of the constituent parts of an organized pattern of activity are of such a nature as to conduce to the perpetuation of the patterned activity, there exists the basis of sensitivity.[17]

And when this is so, it follows that

Responses are not merely selective, but are discriminatory, in behalf of some results rather than others. This discrimination is the essence of sensitivity. Thus with organization, bias becomes interest, and satisfaction a good or value and not a mere satiation of wants or repletion of deficiencies.[18]

Thus it would seem that the most elemental trait in the nature of the human individual is grounded in his very existence as a singularity, and especially in his being alive. It would appear that not only the character of the individual but even his very existence is directly dependent upon his environment.

Individuality itself is originally a potentiality and is realized only in interaction with surrounding conditions. In this process of intercourse, native capacities, which contain an element of uniqueness, are transformed and become a self. Moreover, through resistance encountered, the nature of the self is discovered. The self is both formed and brought to consciousness through interaction with environment.[19]

When it is remembered that such environment includes social, cultural, and personal factors, it becomes apparent that the nature of religious experience, and so of religious values, is directly a function of the social, universal, and cosmic environment in which the individual is interrelated. Such values may be "had" in the inner, ineffable privacy of the individual in his "solitariness"; but they are originated in, shaped by, and sustained through the outer, identifiable, relationships grounded in interactions,

Dewey seems to have been deeply impressed with the significance of this external, uncertain, precarious aspect of the individual's existence. Thus he points out:

The conjunction of problematic and determinate characters in nature renders every existence, as well as every idea and human act, an experiment in fact, even though not in design.[20]

The total bearing of this fact would obviously include every aspect of life and consciousness, so that it is to be expected that man would become somewhat aware of the tentative character of all that he experiences. Dewey is of the opinion that this awareness has been manifested in religious consciousness and thought. He has expressed his understanding in this fashion:

The Christian idea of this world and this life as a probation is a kind of distorted recognition of the situation; distorted because it applied wholesale to one stretch of existence in contrast with another, regarded as original and final. But in truth anything which can exist at any place and at any time occurs subject to tests imposed upon it by surroundings, which are only in part compatible and reinforcing.[21]

Dewey carries his own thought out to its logical conclusion: "Every existence is an event"; and recognizes that this can be very disturbing to the consciousness in matters of affection and esteem, as when he says:

This fact is nothing at which to repine and nothing to gloat over. It is something to be noted and used. If it is discomfiting when applied to good things, to our friends, possessions and precious selves, it is consoling also to know no evil endures forever; the longest lane turns sometime, and the memory of loss of nearest and dearest grows dim in time.[22]

Whatever may be held as to the dogged courage, or candid realism, of such a view, it is possible that here is revealed an intrinsic limitation which characterizes Dewey's philoso-

phical point of view, certainly in this context. Here he does not escape from the temporal shifting, changing scene. There is in this expression no cognizance of the "permanent"—no recognition of the significance of the "final," as so patently occurs in all art: in all consummatory esthetic experience.

In the discussion of the nature of esthetic perception, and of art products, as set forth in his conception of art, it will be noted that the significant quality of such modes of action are precisely involved in the conception of "form," which has the instrumental facility to induce certain immediate final experiences whenever it is brought within the focus of consciousness. Dewey has never attempted to identify "form" beyond pointing to its operational function. For this procedure he has laid down this principle:

Immediate things may be pointed to by words, but not described or defined.[22]

And this is all experimental thinking will ever do about the self, the person, the companion, the friend, God. But this is by no means to discount, nor to deny, the existence of such "event." It is simply to admit the intrinsic technical limitations of thinking that is grounded in the knowledge process.

However limited experimental thinking may be in its description and presentation of such "events" as the individual, the self, it would still seem to suffice for the practical purpose of facilitating the possession of the high values which are grounded in self-consciousness. The sense of value is definitely enhanced by added insight into the practical significance of the self in the course of affairs, which is achieved "with the reflective discovery of the part played in experience by concrete selves, with their ways of acting, thinking, and desiring." Such insight generates "power" "in its ability to distinguish certain conditions of experience," inasmuch as the ability to recognize the nature of the self makes possible the project of manipulating the character of the self that is being achieved. Dewey has described this principle thus:

The change from immediate use in enjoyment and suffering is equivalent to recognition of a method of procedure, and of the alliance of insight into method with possibility of control.[24]

It will be remembered as a basic tenet in Dewey's philosophy that always "a sequential order involves the last term" which points the way to intelligent manipulation since, "in a legitimate account of ends as endings, all directional order resides in the sequential order." Thus it follows that to recognize the self as an "ending" occurring in eventual sequence, as the result of certain antecedent conditions, is both to guide the choices which determine the character which shall be manifested and to invest all the precedent phases of the whole movement with ultimate and final significance.

A direct approach to a close examination of the origin and the nature of the "self" is obscured in Dewey's thought by his obvious aversion to the acceptance of any "structure" as a permanent, immutable thing. Despite his avowed insight that nature includes both the temporary and the final, in his discussion of "existence," Dewey leans so decidedly toward the universality of "change," that while he admits "structure" as "constancy of means," and defines "construction" as "an evident order of changes," he does not ever make a separate entity of this "evident order." That this "order" possesses unique form, identifiable, cognizable, would seem to be what constitutes it "evident"; and, in his analysis of art as experience, Dewey takes such "order" as intrinsic in perception. Yet at this point there

is a definite unwillingness to turn this order into a meta-physical substance. Dewey's intent is indicated when he comments:

The name (structure) designates a character in operation, not an entity.[25]

There need be no impatience with Dewey's zeal to avoid metaphysical substantiation of "structure"; but there is difficulty in understanding the emphasis with which unique actuality is denied to an existence which is analytically discriminable. The interest of this discussion in this phase of Dewey's thought is generated in the premise wherein the "self" is regarded as a *structure*. To deny actuality to "structure" as such is to prejudice all consideration of value or process wherein the "self" is held to be an integral element or factor. But that Dewey does not *mean* to deny "existence" in structure would seem to be clear in this statement which is found in the immediate context.

That structure, whether of the kind called material or of the kind summed up in the word mental, is stable or permanent relationally and in its office, may be shown in another way.[26]

From this it would appear that Dewey's discussion of the inconstancy of structure was aimed to refute any claimed "substantiality" but not actual "reality."

That such a conclusion is sound, as being consonant with Dewey's further thought in this field, is indicated by his elaboration of the "objective" aspect of "form." In a brilliant analysis of the course of Greek philosophy, Dewey offers an explanation of the classic interest in "form."

Form was the first and last word of philosophy because it had been that of art; form is change arrested in a prerogative object. It conveys a sense of the imperishable and timeless, although the material in which it is exemplified is subject to decay and contingency.[27]

Here would be an entirely adequate description of the nature of the "self"; for, while Dewey's explanation accounts for the emergence of the concept of "form," it by no means disposes of it as being ephemeral or unreal. The proclivity to assume that to "explain" means to "explain away" has persistently hounded philosophy in the common thinking of the common people; but it need not prompt an erroneous conclusion here. It belongs again to an experimental approach to keep in mind that whereas analysis and interpretation make for better understanding, and genetic description of the nature of an object provides the basis for criticism and improvement, such procedures could not if they would, and would not if they could, despoil the values which man has had.

That the "self" is to be held as objective and real, is supported by the fact that it may properly be held as a legitimate "matter of science." Dewey states:

The matter of science is a character of natural events and changes as they change: their character of regular and stable order.[28]

Thus he has laid the basis for a deliberate experimental investigation of the "self," about which no more need be claimed than that it is a specific "character of regular and stable order." Apparently there can be no objection to conceiving the "self" as "matter" in the scientific use of that term. Again, Dewey observes:

Matter expresses their (natural events) sequential order, and mind the order of their meanings in their logical connections and dependencies.[29]

On this basis, the "self" as an event in the course of events is to be taken as "material" rather than "mental." By way of illustrating his thought, Dewey remarks:

A curve is an intelligible object.[30]

Now, since a "curve" is obviously a matter of "form," a "structure," it apparently follows that "structures" are "intelligible objects" with "properties" involved in their meanings. And so the idea is further sustained that the "self" is a proper "object" to be examined in intelligent reflection.

When it is recalled that

The character of the object is like that of a tool, say a lever; it is an order of determination of sequential changes terminating in a foreseen consequence,[31]

the significance of understanding and regulating the "self," in its bearing upon the weal and woe of human experience, become quite obvious. Such understanding is by no means to be taken as a neutral affair, or as an idle matter. It belongs to the experimental interpretation of human consciousness to hold that all thinking is directly and normally involved in the actual living process of the thinker. Thus it appears to follow that self-consciousness, or the perception of the self, has a practical bearing upon the self and through the self upon the whole world. Dewey's argument is not too obvious, but his conclusion seems to be firmly held: and he does not hesitate to draw further conclusions from that as a premise.

The very fact that events now past are what they were in their eventual context, and so cannot be altered, seems sufficient ground to find that all perception of the self, all self-consciousness, is necessarily based upon anticipation of the future. It is just because the future is not yet settled that it can be "perceived." Dewey states it thus:

Unless there were something problematic, undecided, still going-on and as yet unfinished and indeterminate, in nature, there could be no such events as perceptions.[32]

This is consistent with Dewey's general conception of any "idea": it invariably has a forward reference. So that it

is to be recognized as typically experimental to understand
that my concept of the "self," my own or any other person's,
will be grounded in terms of what I judge that individual
will do in situations that have not yet occurred. This is a
matter of bringing the "future" retroactively into the
interpretation of the present, and so investing the formulation of "expectation," "ideas," at this present moment with
ultimate and final significance. This whole process is
described by Dewey when he writes:

The immediate perceptibility of meanings, the very existence of
ideas, testifies to insertion of the problematic and hazardous in
the settled and uniform, and to the meeting, crossing and
parting of the substantial, static, and the transitive and particular.[33]

In terms of the "self," it is to be understood that the
"problematic and hazardous" points to the future, which
is as yet only tentative, possible, and potential, whereas
"the settled and uniform" points to the past, whose events
as history must forever be as they were. Thus may be felt
the conditions which make self-consciousness so absorbing
and so demanding: not only is the individual of supreme
significance in living, because it belongs to him and to
him alone to choose what the world shall be; but the
present moment, "now," is of unique import because it is
here that the course of the future is determined. Such
considerations support the basic premise of this discussion,
that the highest, most precious values, the religious, are
found in the course of self-consciousness; and that the
greatest significance for the world of tomorrow is lodged
in the intelligent understanding and disposition of the self
today.

The practical bearing of this truth is so vital as to
warrant further elaboration of the principle involved. While
it is always to be remembered that "the world we have

experienced becomes an integral part of the self," so that something of the "meaning and value" of things and events experienced "is retained as an integral part of the self," and such remembrance may well induce a humble sense of dependence upon the world in which we live, there is a distinct challenge and inspiration to dignity and self-respect in the fact that the individual exerts a decisive, determinative bearing upon the course of events in which he participates. That some such reconstruction proceeds continuously seems to be the only conclusion that can be taken as valid. Dewey has implied this when he observed:

The organism brings with it its own structure, native and acquired, forces that play a part in the interaction. The self acts as well as undergoes, and its undergoings are not impressions stamped upon an inert wax but depend upon the way the organism reacts and responds.[34]

Apparently the reconstruction process is not haphazard or mechanical, but is as subject to the operation of intelligence as is any other course of conscious activity. It is a well-known fact that classic philosophy held all "form" to be real, "permanent," "unchangeable," and so "pre-existent," so far as particular manifestations were concerned. It belongs to the logical consistency of Dewey's philosophic system, grounded upon his basic conception of a pluralistic universe, to hold that all relationships and so all structures are attained and developed as events. He observes:

But the notion that action and sentiment are inherently unified in the constitution of human nature has nothing to justify it. Integration is something to be achieved.[35]

He finds support for this observation in the possibility of personality disorganization, since "division of attitude and responses, compartmentalizing of interests, is easily ac-

quired." That such is actually the case is abundantly verified by the growing demands upon psychiatry and psycho-
therapy to achieve some integrative solution for problems
of personality disorder.

It will be helpful to keep in mind that the "self" involves
perception of the role which the individual will perform
in specific situations anticipated by the individual. When
such situations are various, discrete, unrelated, there may
be a multiplicity of "selves" within the consciousness of the
one individual, arousing and stimulating attention in the
several directions. Dewey points out:

We arrive at true conceptions of motivating and interest only
by recognition that selfhood (except it has encased itself in a
shell of routine) is in process of making, and that any self is
capable of including within itself a number of inconsistent
selves, of unharmonized dispositions.[36]

This plurality of "selves," however, is to be understood as a
temporary, inadequate condition, somewhat as a primary
stage in the achievement of personality. Its significance as
testimony of the origin of the self, however, is obvious, as
Dewey has noted:

There is no one ready-made self behind activities. There are
complex, unstable, opposing attitudes, habits, impulses, which
gradually come to terms with one another, and assume a certain
consistency of configuration, even though only by means of a
distribution of inconsistencies which keeps them in water-tight
compartments, giving them separate turns or tricks in action.[37]

Dewey has noted that, empirically, subjective mind is "an
agency of novel reconstruction of a preexisting order."
It is in the "novelty" that the "individual" achieves "character," "individuality." It was pointed out above that,
while Dewey conceives "mind" in general to be the organization of meanings, he conceives each individual as having

a "mind" of his own, unique, free, and to some extent inscrutable and unpredictable. Yet it is something achieved
through group experience, not something inherited, acquired in toto, or preexistent. Thus speaking of "the mind
that appears *in* individuals," he remarks (as was noted
above):

The former is in itself a system of belief, recognitions and
ignorances, or acceptances and rejections, of expectancies and
appraisals of meanings which have been instituted under the
influence of custom and traditions.[88]

But such structure, received in discourse and communication, in social and mental interaction, is part of the "preexisting order" which the subjective mind of the individual
proceeds to "reconstruct" in novel fashion. Dewey emphasizes "the genuinely intermediate position of subjective
mind," holding it to be "a mode of natural existence in
which objects undergo directed reconstitution." It will serve
the purpose of this discussion to note that when the "object"
undergoing "directed reconstitution" is the perception of
the role the individual himself is to perform, the "self" is
being produced.

While the perception of the self is a product of subjective mind, the process involved is directly related to the
external world through the role which the individual per-
forms in his conduct. The perception of the role occurs in
the subjective processes but the performance of that role is
objective, external, practical. As a matter of fact, even the
attainment of perception is objective in its nature. There is
no such thing as an individual becoming aware of "self" in
any immediate, direct fashion. The "self" of which the individual becomes aware is entirely a matter of the individual's participation in the affairs of the external world.
Conduct and consequences are doubtless important in their

own practical bearing upon other events, but at the same time they form, reveal, and test the self. It is just because "conduct" is so preeminently a matter of choice, that it serves so well to reveal the self for what it is, since choice is. the most characteristic activity of the self. While that "choice" may originate within subjective processes, it appears, and is, and operates, only in actual conduct. The dual significance of choice embodied in conduct is manifested in that it reveals the existing self and it forms the future self.

The actual function of "choice" seems to be one aspect of the operation of individual mind in "remaking" the "pre-existent order." Even when no debating of relative merits of alternative possibilities has occurred, as when an individual received a "message" or an "idea" by communication from others, there is something decisive and determinative in a novel sense when he "chooses" to accept as his own that which has been presented to his conscious attention. This is described in some detail as follows:

To say in a significant way, "*I* think, believe, desire, instead of barely *it* is thought, believed, desired," is to accept and affirm a responsibility and put forth a claim. It does not mean that the self is the source or author of the thought and affection nor its exclusive seat. It signifies that the self as a centered organization of energies identifies itself (in the sense of accepting their consequences) with a belief or sentiment of independent and external origination.[30]

The bearing of this insight upon the processes of education, as a corrective to extreme views in rejecting any aim at "transmission" of factual content, based upon the empirical findings of others and the experimental conclusions of research and reflection, is obvious. Economy of time and energy will prompt the sharing with novitiates of the findings as investigators, inventors, explorers, etc. And yet the

point is placed directly upon the significance of the "acceptance": the "gospel" must be "believed" for it to become effective. There must be an actual participation on the part of the individual in terms of commitment in the sense that the individual assumes personal responsibility involving his own fortune and welfare.

To say "*I* think, hope and love" is to say in effect that genesis is not the last word; instead of throwing the blame or the credit for the belief, affection and expectation upon nature, one's family, church or state, one declares one's self to be henceforth a partner. An adoptive act is proclaimed in virtue of which one claims the benefit of future goods and admits liability for future ills flowing from the affair in question.[40]

The full effect of conduct may well extend beyond the range of self-consciousness. Though "choice" is doubtless involved in all action, there doubtless will be occasions when it is being exercised unwittingly. But consequences will always follow, even if they sometimes escape attention. Such are none the less real and vital for being unnoticed. It is probable that at no time can the full sweep of the significance of any act be entirely envisioned. So much must forever lie beyond our ken. But that consequences *do* follow every action, and that they have a bearing upon the self is a truth which belongs pertinently to the discussion in hand.

Whenever anything is undergone in consequence of a doing, the self is modified. The modification extends beyond acquisition of greater facility and skill. Attitudes and interests are built up which embody in themselves some deposit of the meaning of things done and undergone. These funded and retained meanings become a part of the self. They constitute the capital with which the self notes, cares for, attends and purposes.[41]

The self will be formed, and will have consequences quite

apart from the exercise of intelligent reflections; just as
the physical processes will operate with or without the
benefit of mental activity. But, in precisely the same way
as intelligent understanding will serve to improve and
enhance physical activities, so will it operate to advance
the satisfactions and values of self-realization. When once
it is understood how the self is formed, and how it functions,
the enlargement and the improvement of the values involved will follow directly as a matter of course.

Perhaps the most fruitful approach to consideration of
the self from a functional point of view is to take it in its
instrumental aspect as a "tool." Not only does this serve to
identify the process by which it is produced, but it points
directly to the practical potentialities that are involved.
It has been noted that the self is perceived in relation to
possible situations that may arise in the future, involving
the individual as a participant. To conceive it as a "tool" is
to have in mind its directing function in the disposition
of eventual situations:

The invention and use of tools have played a large part in con-
solidating meanings, because a tool is a thing used as means to
consequences, instead of being taken directly and physically. It
is intrinisically relational, anticipatory, predictive. Without
reference to the absent, or "transcendence," nothing is a tool.[4]

In the terms of this comment, the "absent" is the future
situation in which the self is expected to be involved in a
determinative way. The scope of the "transcendence" would
seem to be infinite: anything in which the individual can
conceivably be involved will serve to qualify the "self" as
it is conceived. It is important to keep in mind that such
conception of the "self" is not a matter of investing the
individual organism with any innate or original "powers"
that are to emerge at some future time and place, but it is

an expanding, developing, changing anticipation of the role which the individual will perform in situations which are foreseen as possible. Dewey's remark about the relational aspect of a "tool" is illuminating here:

A tool is a particular thing, but it is more than a particular thing, since it is a thing in which a connection, a sequential bond of nature is embodied. It possesses an objective relation as its own defining property.[42]

It may be noted again that it is precisely this relational nature of the self that constitutes it as a proper "object" of science.

The objects of science, like the direct objects of the arts, are an order of relations which serve as tools to effect immediate havings and beings.[43]

And this is to say that the full application of experimental interpretation and explanation can be confidently directed to the problem of understanding, and so of manipulating the self. The fact that religious values are involved implies no complication whatever. Since "the *ultimate* objects of science are guided processes of change," it is only necessary to conceive the self as a formulated structure, an order of procedure, in which intelligent guidance is operative in origin, review, and revision, to bring the full application of scientific principles to bear upon the management of the self.

However, in the interests of avoiding misunderstanding, an observation as to the nature of such proper "objects of science," though perhaps redundant, may be in proper place here. It is to be kept in mind that the "self" (likewise the "soul," the "spirit," the "individual"), as such an "object," is an abstract "instrument" available to be applied in practical affairs, from the experimental and functional point of view. As such it is to be distinguished from concrete objects, such as "persons," which are events. Further-more, the "self" is to be held as any other structure, a genuine emergent within the matrix of nature. This will give no cause for concern as long as the *instrumental* character of such description is kept in mind. On the con-trary, this view keeps the whole achievement of selfhood suitable for scientific investigation and intelligent manipu-lation. Whatever the "self" is conceived to be, it must be lodged entirely within nature to be significant from the point of view of experimentalism. Dewey has implied this necessity in this general comment about science:

Only as science is seen to be fulfilled and brought to itself in intelligent management of historical processes in their continuity can man be envisaged as within nature, and not as a super-natural extrapolation.[45]

When such "intelligent management of historical processes in their continuity" is seen to be the meaning of the "self," the general importance of the experimental understanding of the processes of self-realization can be clearly felt. Dewey affirms the import of this truth in much stronger vein:

Yet till we understand operations of the self as the tool of tools, *the* means in all use of means, specifying its differential activi-ties in their distinctive consequences in varying qualities of what is experienced, science is incomplete and the use made of it is at the mercy of an unknown factor, so that the ultimate and important consequence is in so far a matter of accident. Inten-tions and efforts bring forth the opposite of what was intended and striven for and the result is confusion and catastrophe.[46]

SOCIETY

The foregoing interpretation of the origin and nature of the "self" noted, in passing, the existence of traits of

"sociability and communication" grounded in "affinities and active outreachings for connection and intimate union" in the individual. There is an inescapable impression of ambivalence in all that marks human nature: the "individual existence has a double status and import."

> There is the individual that belongs in a continuous system of connected events which reinforce its activities and which form a world in which it is at home, consistently at one with its own preferences, satisfying its requirements . . . . Then there is the individual that finds a gap between its distinctive bias and the operations of the things through which alone its need can be satisfied; it is broken off, discrete, because it is at odds with its surroundings.[7]

This twofold development seems to follow from the disparity implicit in the axial structure of all experience: the organism, operating "through its own structure" toward integration of activity in satisfaction of its vital needs; and the environment, impinging upon the organism to stimulate, irritate, disturb, provoke reaction and adjustment which become change, alteration, growth. Here may be seen the basic pattern of the individual and the group. Even the individual is to be understood in this double sense: as one in his own unique existence and as one of the group. The terms "self" and "society" may well be used to denote, on the one hand, the individual identity as he appears in his own consciousness, and on the other hand, the group in which the individual has the "status and import" assigned to him by others. It is important to keep in mind the functional character of those terms. No metaphysical implications or denotations are insinuated.

Genetically, experience occurs in individuals, but the social situation which grounds, develops, and sustains the "self" is actually constituted by the propinquity of a plurality of persons and the process of "the peculiar form

which interaction sometimes assumes in the case of human
beings," known as communication. The occurrence of such
situations is entirely within the scope of natural events from
a philosophical point of view, since

nature is seen to be marked by histories, some of which terminate in the existence of human beings, and finally in their
intelligent activities.[48]

In so far as "communication" is involved in "intelligent
activity" of "human beings," this operation is well within
nature and so can be identified in natural terms. Com-
menting more definitely, Dewey remarks:

In experience, human relations, institutions and traditions are
as much a part of the nature in which and by which we live
as is the physical world. Nature in this meaning is not "outside."
It is in us and we are in it and of it.[49]

This rather neutral description denotes what Dewey intends by the "intelligent activities" of "human beings."
Nothing more definite was needed for the purpose Dewey
had in mind when he distinguishes man from animal, but
Dewey's use of the word "natural" is not meant to exclude
the "religious"; and his use of the term "human" as a special
form of natural events is not to be construed as excluding
reference to "man—God" relations, since there seems to be
no logical necessity to confine Dewey's terms in categories
more differentiated than the context implies.

The original condition of the process of communication
is in itself nothing remarkable, since "the catching up of
human individuals into association" is but "a manifestation
of a commonplace of existence." However, "significance
resides not in the bare fact of association," "but in the
consequences that flow from the distinctive patterns of
human association." At this point Dewey notes as a general
observation:

The significant consideration is that assemblage of organic human beings transforms sequence and coexistence into participation.[50]

This comment would indicate that "participation" is to be taken as the "significant" aspect of human "association," and to this conclusion the following excerpt of discussion seems to point in clearest fashion.

It is also an obvious empirical fact that animals are connected with each other in inclusive schemes of behavior by means of signaling acts, in consequence of which certain acts and consequences are deferred until a joint action made possible by the signaling occurs. In the human being, this function becomes language, communication, discourse, in virtue of which the consequences of the experience of one form of life are integrated in the behavior of others. With the development of recorded speech, the possibilities of this integration are indefinitely widened—in principle the cycle of objective integration within the behavior of a particular organism is completed. Not merely its own distinct world of spacetime is involved in its conduct but the world of its fellows. When consequences which are unexperienced and future to one agent are experienced and past to another creature with which it is in communication, organic prudence becomes conscious expectation, and future affairs living present realities. Human learning and habit forming present thereby an integration of organic-environmental connections so vastly superior to those of animals without language that its experience appears to be superorganic.[51]

The full import of this insight can scarcely be measured, since it provides for an undestanding of the processes involved in the achieving and the distribution of the greatest values possible for man. This is readily demonstrated when the principle indicated is applied in description of that form of religious experience which in history has been called "Christian." The fact that language, as "recorded speech," implements communication among persons separated by space and time, makes it possible to apprehend the practical potentialities claimed in the Christian system, in which it is held that while grounding their satisfactions and joys in the fellowship and communion mutually shared by the contemporary believers and their absent Lord, the acceptance of the "Holy Scriptures" as the authentic revelation in "recorded speech" of the "mind of Christ" facilitates actual communication and participation in a mode of living designated as "Eternal Life." Dewey had something less specific in mind when he wrote:

Of all affairs, communication is the most wonderful. That things should be able to pass from the plane of external pushing and pulling to that of revealing themselves to man, and thereby to themselves; and that the fruit of communication should be participation, sharing, is a wonder by the side of which transubstantiation pales.[52]

The practical results of this process are varied and important in human affairs. Something of its function in enriching the bare events of organic environmental interaction is indicated in this comment:

Where communication exists, things in acquiring meaning, thereby acquire representatives, surrogates, signs and implicates, which are infinitely more amenable to management, more permanent and more accommodating, than events in their first estate.[53]

Thus it serves as "a natural bridge that joins the gap between existence and essence," and by its operation in establishing "meanings" is directly responsible for the emergence of "mind." In this it distinguishes man from animal by facilitating the manifestation of "such intrinsic differences as religions, art and science, industry and politics."

The process of "communication" involves "connec-

tions," but these are not to be limited to such as exist in "the original gross experience of things."

Connection is instituted through operations which define ideas, and operations are as much matters of experience as are sensory qualities.[54]

This recognition of the validity of the empirical results of ideal operations provides the basis for the extension of the range of communication and its consequences to infinite possibilities in nonexistential realities. The authentic character of such extension is supported by this further word from Dewey:

To the original gross experience of things there is superadded another type of experience, the product of deliberate art, of which relations rather than qualities are the significant subject matter. These connections are as much experienced as are the qualitatively diverse and irreducible objects of original natural experiences.[55]

It would appear that the "meanings" which constitute "mind" are actually "connections" instituted by operational behavior. Though the process of production is obscure, Dewey has no doubt of its authenticity. Thus he writes:

Meaning is not indeed a psychic existence; it is primarily a property of behavior, and secondarily a property of objects. But the behavior of which it is a quality is a distinctive behavior; cooperative, in that response to another's act involves contemporaneous response to a thing as entering into the other's behavior, and this upon both sides. It is difficult to state the exact physiological mechanism which is involved. But about the fact there is no doubt.[56]

Thus it would seem that not only is "meaning" a property of operational behavior but also that such behavior is necessarily "cooperative" in the course of "organized interaction" between "feeling creatures" on the level of "language, communication." The further fact that "language, or some form of artificial signs serves to register the relationship" grounded in such communal activity, and to "make it fruitful in other contexts of particular existence," points to the instrumental role of communication in securing and in sharing human goods.

This is to be recognized in the achievement of the highest forms of distinctively human goods.

Culture is the product not of efforts of men put forth in a void or just upon themselves, but of prolonged and cumulative interaction with environment.[57]

This "environment" consists of other human beings involved in cooperative action. Dewey does not hesitate to insist that such group participation is a categoric necessity.

A society or some specific group of fellow men, is always accessory before and after the fact . . . . Neutrality is non-existent. Conduct is always shared; this is the difference between it and a physiological process. It is not an ethical "ought" that conduct *should* be social. It *is* social, whether good or bad.[58]

Nor does he shrink from pressing this principle to apply to the whole range of conscious conduct. Thus he writes:

The stuff of belief and proposition is not originated by us. It comes to us from others, by education, tradition, and the suggestion of the environment. Our intelligence is bound up, so far as its materials are concerned, with the community of life of which we are a part. We know what it communicates to us, and know according to the habits it forms in us. Science is an affair of civilization not of individual intellect.[59]

Not only knowledge, but moral judgment is likewise to be so understood as a product of communal interaction.

So with conscience . . . . In language and imagination we rehearse the responses of others just as we dramatically enact other consequences. We foreknow how others will act, and the

foreknowledge is the beginning of judgment passed on action. We know *with* them; there is conscience.[60]

The direct bearing of the cultural complex in the development of the character of the individual seems clearly indicated in this insight into the process of communication. It is apparent that society is not introduced or imposed from without, nor is it brought to bear upon man as a desirable influence: rather, it is involved in his existence.

Social interaction is not only operative in thus producing the instrumental structure of the individual, known as his "character," but it functions in his having and enjoying the consummations which comprise his most precious values.

Communication is consummatory as well as instrumental. It is a means of establishing cooperation, domination and order. Shared experience is the greatest of human goods. In communication, such conjunction and contact as is characteristic of animals become endearments capable of infinite idealization; they become symbols of the very culmination of nature. That God is love is a more worthy idealization than that the divine is power. Since love at its best brings illumination and wisdom, this meaning is as worthy as that the divine is truth.[61]

While it has been noted that communication serves as a vital process in the enriching of human experience by facilitating "cooperative" action and mutual sharing and participation on the level of "organized interaction" between autonomous individual organic units of energy, it remains to be noted that it is incidental to the achievement of a still higher plane of experience generating even greater and more precious values. Dewey suggests how this further significance could easily be overlooked:

Communication through speech, oral and written, is the familiar and constant feature of social life. We tend, accordingly, to regard it as just one phenomenon among others of what we must in any case accept without question. We pass over the fact that it is the foundation and source of all activities and relations that are distinctive of internal union of human beings with one another.[62]

The nature of this "internal union" is probably grounded in the process of communication itself. Dewey has noted:

Such is the essence and import of communication, signs and meaning. Something is literally made common in at least two different centers of behavior. To understand is to anticipate together, it is to make a cross-reference which, when acted upon, brings about a partaking in a common, inclusive undertaking.[63]

This results in

the establishment of cooperation in an activity in which there are partners, and in which the activity of each is modified and regulated by partnership.[64]

It may well be noted here that such "partnership" in its very nature exists "by faith," that kind of faith in which confidence is placed in the "intention" of the other. The intrinsic necessity for "communication" as a vehicle for the sharing of "intent and purpose" points to the requirement of some medium of art as a condition for the maintenance of community, in which the goods of "friendship and intimate affection" are to be had. Dewey has commented on the nature of such communion in these words:

It is when the desires and aims, the interests and modes of response of another become an expansion of our own being that we understand him.[65]

And yet it would seem that something still more mutual is actually achieved: not so much a matter of "identification" on the part of one who enters into the pattern of being of the other, as a matter of realization of actual community as a structure of relationships in which the

self is grounded and to which it belongs. Dewey feels that such is a common experience.

Within the flickering inconsequential acts of separate selves dwells a sense of the whole which claims and dignifies them."

It would seem that by communication such "a sense" could become the common consciousness of the participants and thus provide for the enhancement and the sharing of the values achieved.

It remains to be noted that the implementation of such social intercourse is by art, of which language is the eminent form. Dewey has pointed out that

The expressions that constitute art are communication in its pure and undefiled form. Art breaks through barriers that divide human beings, which are impermeable in ordinary association. This force of art, common to all the arts, is most fully manifested in literature."

This comment helps to understand the great importance of so-called sacred writings in the history of religion. Implementation of communication, of social intercourse, is generally established, systematized, and stereotyped in the customs, institutions, and traditions which comprise the culture of any given group or society.

The effect of society's impress upon the individual in the way of guiding his activities is definitive. Not only is the existence of his mind dependent upon "shared undertakings" invoking others, but even the operation of intelligence is significantly conditioned.

When we begin to forecast consequence, the consequences that most stand out are those which will proceed from other people. The resistance and the cooperation of others is the central fact in the furtherance or failure of our schemes."

Apparently this function of society extends with ever increasing import throughout the whole range of human affairs. It enables the average school child to employ competently knowledge that Copernicus and Galileo did not have, and guides the least member of society along ways that are good, far beyond his own capacity to recognize or to appreciate.

Thus the ultimate buttress of the soundness of all but the simplest ideas consists in the cumulative objective appliances and arts of the community, not in anything found in "consciousness" itself or within the organism."[69]

It is "the desire to be in harmony with others" that leads a person to fall in with prevailing ideas, even prejudices as well as beliefs, of others; and which serves as one of the conditions which make education practicable. In a very real sense this willingness of the pupil to be taught is matched by the desire of society, through teaching, to perpetuate the existent social order by inculcating its character in the mind of the pupil. The dangers in thus conditioning the pupil in a cultural pattern formulated in other, prior, situations, which may prove a hindrance to efficient manipulation of his present affairs, are real and great, but by no means simple or absolute. The benefits of such training are at the same time just as considerable, and far more significant. It is at this point that intelligence in pedagogy is so extremely important: techniques of inquiry, facts of discovery, ideals of goods, are transmissible through educational processes grounded in this very relationship.

Everything the teacher does, as well as the manner in which he does it, incites the child to respond in some way or other, and each response tends to set the child's attitude in some way or other."[70]

BELIEF

One of the distinctive qualities of experience on the human level is its capacity to become conscious of itself.

Under the conditions of social existence human affairs tend to produce structures of mind, self, and society as organizations of meaning, energy, and custom. As an integral development in this social process, acts of commitment, belief structures, occur grounded in judgment, construed in intent, and activated in consent. "Habits of belief" are being formed constantly as men live and deal with each other, thereby rendering present experience more significant as personal commitment adds determinative direction.

Knowing, believing, involves something additive and extrinsic to having a meaning.[71]

Just as "any idea as such designates an operation that *may* be performed, not something in actual existence," even so, in its logical structure "a belief refers to something beyond itself by which its value may be tested; it makes an assertion about some matter of fact, or some principle or law." In operation a belief employs a technique similar to thinking, leading again to the indefinite enrichment of the significance of common experience.

When activity is directed by distant things, contact activities must be inhibited or held in. They become instrumental; they function only as far as needed to direct the distance-conditioned activities.[72]

Thus any complex of immediate experience can become more and more meaningful, when, by virtue of belief, the immediate activities are instrumental in achieving distant and refined goods.

Dewey recognizes "two modes, two dimensions of belief," and has described them thus:

Man has beliefs which scientific inquiry vouchsafes, beliefs about the actual structure and processes of things; and he also has beliefs about the values which should regulate his conduct.[73]

Such discrimination is doubtless valid for the argument there in hand, but there seems room for question as to its adequacy in view of Dewey's thought as set forth elsewhere. Would not this twofold aspect tend to disappear as man is held impersonally to be a natural event? In line with the general analysis made in naturalistic humanism, do not the human and the natural, ethics and science, blend as one? Is there not a more real cleavage suggested by Dewey in his analysis of nature in *Experience and Nature,* as between the regular and the unique aspects of natural events, pointing to differences in beliefs as between conformity and originality, the uniform and the spontaneous? This would distinguish the beliefs which man holds as a matter of consensus from the beliefs which a man holds independently and responsibly as a matter of choice, even more or less consciously unique.

A further question as to the adequacy of this twofold distinction might well be raised. Granted that there are "beliefs about actual existences and the course of events," such as would be based upon experimental investigation of subject matter in hand, and "beliefs about ends to be striven for, policies to be adopted, goods to be attained, and evils to be averted," such as would be based upon ethical evaluation of possibilities in view, should there not be recognized a third class of beliefs? Both classes of belief described conceive the validity of the confidence involved to be grounded in the efficient actions of the human organism, in what man has competently observed and wisely chosen. As such they seem to be similarly distinctly individualistic, and so do not seem to provide adequate description for the type of belief generated in social experience, where the focus of attention is upon mutual goods to be secured by social action, communal action. There are activities of this sort, which an indi-

vidual cannot perform alone, and which are in themselves
more than merely additive enlargement of volume and
scope due to a plurality of participants. Such are actions
which intrinsically involve togetherness, dependent upon
mutual consent, trust, and commitment; actions which require belief by one partner in the intent or will of the
other. However much such belief may be bolstered by factual record, and confirmed by logical reflection, there is
a determinative element which remains inscrutably resident
in the spontaneous individuality of the other person, in
his purpose, his intent, which he can decide, thus know,
and so announce. There is an element of volition which he
can communicate in discourse, which the other can hear,
and, at his own risk, believe. The basis for his confidence
in this belief is not altogether discoverable by investigation,
nor is it entirely valuable by appraisal. It includes a part
that is inscrutable to any such investigation, but which
is attainable by communication. The partners can share
their desires, share their intentions, share their joint decision. In such act of faith each commits his fortune and welfare in the issue at stake upon the integrity of the other.
Whether this kind of belief is sufficiently distinctive to
warrant a third category being recognized is not too important, but that this particular form of belief involving
social process be recognized is very important to an
understanding of the operation of belief in religious experience. Perhaps the thought here could be pointed clearly
by noting that whereas the two classes named by Dewey,
as quoted above, indicate on the one hand beliefs about
existences and events, and on the other beliefs about ends
and goods, there could well be recognized a third class of
beliefs about persons and purposes.

Concepts or ideas of persons involve a greater proportion of belief than concepts of other things. It was

noted earlier in this discussion that all concepts have
their significant, dynamic aspect in their forward bearing
upon the future. Every idea points ahead to what will
follow if certain action is taken. This future element is
in the very nature of the case as yet unsettled and somewhat undetermined. Something will occur. It is the content of belief that the eventual will be such and so.
When the object of belief involves a person there is always
the additional element of that spontaneous, unpredictable,
uncontrollable individuality, not only in any living thing
as a center of unique existence, but even more infinitely in
the will or intent of that person. To have an idea of a
person is not only to believe that such a thing exists but to
believe certain expectations about that being's character,
intention, and purpose. When men say, "I do not feel that
I know that man," they imply, "I cannot as yet anticipate
what he will do." The simple explanation of such "unbelief"
may well be that the other has not indicated or communicated his intent. Thus the first man cannot confidently
expect any specific, given results or eventual developments.
As soon as there is, from observation of characteristic conduct, or from revelation as from the other of his settled
purpose, such confident expectation, there is a readiness
to say "I *know* him," which is to say "I *know* what to *expect*
of him."

The fact that such assertion does not claim immediate
possession of the "person," but rather admits the concept
to be based on inference, dialectically conceived and
logically construed. does not imply any serious defect.
It has been repeatedly noted in this discussion that Dewey's
empirical approach bypasses the problems of metaphysical
existence and nature without prejudice as to whatever
reality or significance may be there involved. The notorious requests for proof or logical demonstration, so widely

and persistently publicized by intellectual skeptics, which have embarrassed sincere believers who claimed direct communication from God, and have harassed others who felt the legitimacy of such claims, in view of the affirmations to which they seemed to be committed, are simply tabled as *not apropos*, in so far as these requests refer to God as a substance, or to God's nature in terms of metaphysical reality. This is not to imply or to concede that God is any less or any different than He has always been. But it is to hold that any conception of Him, grounded in empirical events as had in man's experience, may be rational in origin, without being in the least invalidated or impaired thereby. It will be recalled that Dewey has noted a modal delimitation in scientific method in which the "human meanings of the consequences of natural interactions" are legitimately "passed over." Certainly this did not commit the natural scientist to discount human values. It is perhaps no presumption to reserve the same liberty for religious processes, and thus to hold that to pass over the present lack of knowledge of all the practical ramifications of any belief while enjoying the immediate qualities which contemplation brings to view is also legitimate, even "indispensable." To hold that such beliefs must eventually be sustained in actual operational verification is just as proper as to hold that science must eventually serve the common welfare and minister to the highest human interests of man in order to be finally warranted. Such position can be maintained with fullest sincerity and complete integrity in religion as in science.

The meaningful ground of belief enters the mind as "a deposit of prior experience, personal and communal."

The materials of his thought and belief come to him from others with whom he lives.[74]

But the formation of the belief depends upon a spontaneous element. It "involves personal factors," "a phase of acquiescence," in which the individual "adopts" the possible belief as his own. The following excerpts cited above may be noted again in this connection:

> To say in a significant way, "*I* think, believe, desire, instead of barely *it* is thought, believed, desired," is to accept and affirm a responsibility and to put forth a claim. It does not mean that the self is the source or author of the thought and affection nor its exclusive seat. It signifies that the self as a centered organization of energies identifies itself (in the sense of accepting their consequences) with a belief or sentiment of independent and external origination . . . .
>
> To say "*I* think, hope and love" is to say in effect that genesis is not the last word; instead of throwing the blame or the credit for the belief, affection and expectation upon nature, one's family, church, or state, one declares one's self to be henceforth a partner. An adoptive act is proclaimed in virtue of which one claims the benefit of future goods and admits liability for future ills flowing from the affair in question.[75]

It is this intrinsic forward reference in the act of believing that places such premium upon intelligence as a guiding factor, and upon integrity and persistence as practical conditions, in the securing of the goods to which the belief lays claim.

Any belief as such is tentative, hypothetical; it is not just to be acted upon, but is to be *framed* with reference to its office as a guide to action.[76]

For this, basic knowledge is important.

But these expressions of our nature need *direction,* and direction is possible only through knowledge. When they are informed by knowledge, they themselves constitute, in their directed activity, intelligence in operation.[77]

The structural affinit

reflected in this comment emphasizes the great natural significance of the operation of intelligence in the course of religious experience.

Because beliefs do involve man so completely in their consequences, the importance of careful investigation into the grounds of their claims to acceptance would seem to be in order. But as a matter of fact a large portion of belief as held and exercised by man remains unchallenged in any case.

When all is said and done, the field of fact open to any one observer by himself is narrow. Into every one of our beliefs, even those that we have worked out under the conditions of utmost personal, first-hand acquaintance, much has insensibly entered from what we have heard or read of the observations and conclusions of others.[78]

It is a matter of much good fortune for man that despite such casual, uncritical acceptance, the inherent soundness of correct beliefs benefits the believers apart from any verification.

Even today correct beliefs about the constitution of nature are held by the great multitude merely because they are current and popular, rather than because the multitude understands the reasons upon which they rest.[79]

Man has a natural disposition to adopt beliefs held by persons with prestige, but this is not a tendency that can be followed blindly to advantage.

Reverence for parents and regard for those placed in authority are in the abstract surely valuable traits. Yet, as Locke points out, they are among the chief forces that determine beliefs apart from and even contrary to the operations of intelligent thought. The desire to be in harmony with others is itself a desirable trait. But it may lead a person too readily to fall in with the prejudices of others and may weaken his independence of judgment. It even leads to extreme partisanship that regards it as disloyal to question the beliefs of a group to which it belongs.[80]

Intelligent circumspection in the matter of accepting and holding beliefs will guard against being misled, but there is a yet more positive benefit which rewards diligence in reflection.

Intellectual responsibility secures integrity; that is to say, consistency and harmony in belief.[81]

The arduous nature of intellectual labor discourages some and inclines them toward an easier, more pleasant course.

A judgment as an act of controlled inquiry demands a rich background and a disciplined insight. It is much easier to "tell" people what they should believe than to discriminate and unify. An audience that is itself habituated to being told, rather than schooled in thoughtful inquiry, likes to be told.[82]

Doubtless this is the personal lot of many men, and perhaps it is an inevitable one; but the practical implications are none the less crucial. It is from such self-indulgence that the twin blemishes of dogmatism and skepticism are generated.

Love for security, translated into desire not to be disturbed and unsettled, leads to dogmatism, to acceptance of beliefs upon authority, to intolerance and fanaticism on one side and to irresponsible dependence and sloth on the other.[83]

Skepticism that is not such a search (for new facts and ideas) is as much a personal emotional indulgence as is dogmatism.[84]

In the nature of some cases, beliefs point to consequences which lie beyond the reach of empirical examination. Here there is no direct protection against error.

When there is no direct appreciable reaction of the inference upon the security and prosperity of life, there are no natural checks to the acceptance of wrong beliefs.[85]

This may account for the large content of questionable material in religious beliefs, as evidenced by obvious contradictions both within the single systems and between the several systems as held.

The transcendental reference in so much of religious faith removes the beliefs in question beyond the pale of direct experimental verification, but pragmatic examination proceeds by the mutually dependent processes of practice and logic.

Testing is of two kinds. Suggested inferences are tested in thought to see whether different elements in the suggestion are coherent with one another. They are also tested, after one has been adopted, by *action* to see whether the consequences that are anticipated in *thought* occur in fact.[56]

Apparently such logical test come first, serving instrumentally to the establishing of hypothetical conclusions, which are supported by the demonstration of fitness and coherence within the whole perspective of the individual's life orientation. Here may be noted in passing, the possible ground for the validity of creedal formulations. But such considerations cannot be final in the problem of validity of belief. On the basis of original and formal characteristics alone, discrimination is impossible.

Apart from considerations of use and history there are no original and inherent differences between valid meanings and meanings occurring in revery, desiring, fearing, remembering, all being *intrinsically* the same in relation to events.[57]

As with other ideas, only the pragmatic test will serve.

The fact is that an idea, intellectually, cannot be defined by its structure, but only by its function and use.[58]

It is a matter of practical import that Dewey thinks its application is both possible and necessary.

We have at last reached a point where social conditions create a mind capable of scientific outlook and inquiry. To foster and develop this spirit is the social obligation of the present because it is the urgent need.[89]

Because "it makes all the difference in the world in the value of a belief how its object is formed and arrived at," the "critical valuation" of "immediate belief values" should "proceed in terms of the generation and consequences" of such belief objects: a procedure that affords full opportunity to employ scientific methods of experimental inquiry.

Properties and relations that *entitle* an object to be found good in belief are extraneous to the qualities that are its immediate good; they are casual, and hence found only by research into the antecedent and the eventual.[90]

Here it is apparent that the operation of intelligence functions to produce warrantable results.

When the question is raised as to the "real" value of the object for belief, the appeal is to criticism, intelligence. And the court of appeal decides by the law of conditions and consequences. Inquiry duly pursued leads to the enstatement of an object which is directly accepted, good in belief, but an object whose character now depends upon the reflective operations whose conclusion it is. Like the object of dogmatic and uncritical belief, it marks an "end," a static arrest; but unlike it, the "end" is a *conclusion*: hence it carries credentials.[91]

In the course of self-consciousness, belief is involved in the individual's perception of his own future, his ultimate destiny. Whatever idea of himself he will embrace is necessarily a matter of belief. In so far as he commits himself to that belief he sees himself in the ultimate phase of his own career as the person he will henceforth hold himself to be. The last term in a series qualifies all preceding terms. Herein is to be seen the retroactive present import of the telic element in a man's belief involving himself. The

bearing this will have upon conduct will be a function of the sincerity of conviction in the belief, as well as a manifestation of the integrity of the personality of the individual involved, and of the intelligence operative in his behavior. The notorious uncertainty of the future poses a problematic situation, challenging thought and only to be resolved by deliberate choice. When that choice is made with assurance and held with confident expectation of eventual fortune and felicity, there will be an experience of peace, satisfaction, and joy which will constitute value in the consciousness of the man. It belongs to the common course of human experience that the greatest values are derived through beliefs which generate religious experience.

VALUE

Human experience not only produces patterns of commitment in the course of self-realization, as beliefs, but also arrives at conclusions of judgment in the course of satisfaction, as values. Attention to matters of enjoyment and suffering seems to be a function of man's biological predicament in his "uncertain invironment." "Values of some sort or other" are seen to occur "whenever any object is welcomed and lingered over," or "whenever it arouses aversion and protest," where they appear as "immediate goods of enjoyment and conduct." However, the function of intelligence in operations of judgment is an essential condition for the emergence of values as such.

Dewey decries the thought that any "directly present" quality could ever be "the whole of the thing." There is always "something to be investigated." "Without the intervention of thought," enjoyments are "but problematic goods," and become "values" only "when they reissue in a changed form from intelligent behavior."

There is no value except where there is satisfaction, but there have to be certain conditions fulfilled to transform a satisfaction into a value.[92]

As a matter of fact the bare enjoyment of suffering in itself is something ineffable. Such is a thing "immediately having certain intrinsic qualities," about which "there is accordingly nothing to be said: it is what it is." Of such things Dewey points out:

All that can be said of them concerns their generative conditions and the consequences to which they give rise.[93]

And yet, in their immediate existence, "satisfaction" and "sufferings" constitute the raw material of what should be esteemed and secured. It is taken to be the social task of philosophic criticism to aid the common man in the attainment of preferred values, and this contribution is made "by taking cognizance of their causes and consequences."

It is not the degree of immediate esthetic feeling that constitutes the value of any satisfaction, nor is it some preestablished status assigned in absolutist designation of reality; but "value is determined by the outcome" of operations which investigate the relational connectedness of the immediate satisfaction which is had.

Values (to sum up) may be connected inherently with liking, and yet not with *every* liking but only with those that judgment has approved, after examination of the relation upon which the object liked depends. A casual liking is one that happens without knowledge of how it occurs nor to what effect. The difference between it and one which is sought because of a judgment that it is worth having and is to be striven for, makes just the difference between enjoyments which are accidental and enjoyments that have value and hence a claim upon our attitude and conduct.[94]

Thus values are seen to be products of human activity. It follows that "operational thinking needs to be supplied to the judgment of values," and for this "the funded products of much thoughtful experience," as "operative good judgment and taste," have instrumental significance.

Propositions about what is or has been liked are of instrumental value in reaching judgments of value, in as far as the conditions and consequences of the thing liked are thought about.[95]

Since value is thus determined "by enjoyments which are the consequences of intelligent action," values are taken "to be identical with goods that are the fruit of intelligently directed activity." These observations serve to point to the nature of values as empirical and operational, rather than metaphysical; and stress the fact they may be real and significant even though they are held without other than empirical support and may not be construed as purely rational forms or essences. This remark is not designed to provide ground for holding that religious values are characteristically irrational or illogical, but to note that, as such, religious values may be valid even though their ontological status remains undetermined. At the same time it should be noted that a premium is placed upon the operation of intelligence in the judgmental process as it produces both knowledge and "taste."

Judgment of satisfactions "by means of the relations under which they occur" is "the alternative to definition, classification, and systematization of satisfactions just as they happen to occur," and produces more meaningful, valid, wholesome results. Such judgments also constitute the conditions for the enhancement of appreciation, thus increasing value.

The judgment of the value of an object to be experienced is instrumental to appreciation of it when it is realized.[96]

Inasmuch as they focus consideration forward upon the future, they operate to orient the outlook of man to the "possible" in his affairs.

The relation between objects as known and objects with respect to value is that between the actual and the possible. The "actual" consists of given conditions; the "possible" denotes ends or consequences not now existing, but which the actual may through its use bring into existence.[97]

Dewey's great respect for the significance of man enhances the importance of the problem of values.

The thing which concerns all of us as human beings is precisely the greatest attainable security of value in concrete existence.[98]

It is this practical issue which indicates this phase of the operation of intelligence to have supreme importance.

The significance of intelligence in the formation of value inheres in the importance of "method and means," which is taken to be equal to that of "ends" in "the experimental way of thinking." Dewey has pointed out:

The chief consideration in achieving concrete security of values lies in the perfecting of *methods* of actions.[99]

Hence the need for constant improvement of method by processes of intelligent revision appears as a matter of course. Even when the judgmental function is exercised intuitively as it often is in the form of "direct habits," operating "in direct appraisals of value," this is but "the result of past experience funded into direct outlook upon the scene of life;" as a matter of fact, "intuitions" are all the better for being subjected to such appraisal of their validity as intelligence would direct and perform.

Every intuition, even the best, is likely to become perfunctory and second-hand unless revitalized by consideration of its

meaning—that is, of the consequences that will accrue from acting upon it.[100]

Such direct exercise of judgment is manifest in the operation of "taste," whose practical function is most significant in the process of value judgment.

Cultivated taste alone is capable of prolonged appreciation of the same object; and it is capable of it because it has been trained to a discriminating procedure which constantly uncovers in the ·object new meanings to be perceived and enjoyed.[101]

It is the utilitarian import of values, "using that word to designate whatever is taken to have rightful authority in the direction of conduct," that makes the matter of acquiring "taste" of first importance.

Taste, if we use the word in its best sense, is the outcome of experience brought cumulatively to bear on the intelligent appreciation of the real worth of likings and enjoyments. There is nothing in which a person so completely reveals himself as in the things which he judges enjoyable and desirable.

The formation of a cultivated and effectively operative good judgment or taste with respect to what is esthetically admirable, intellectually acceptable, and morally approvable is the supreme task set to human beings by the incidents of experience.[102]

Value producing situations appear grounded in "some need" of the individual, and develop empirically in the satisfactions or the sufferings undergone, as the individual consciously notes the antecedents and the consequences of such experiences of satisfaction. While such "needs" may be grounded genetically in organic experience, the description of the nature of values as set forth in the thought of John Dewey does not require obvious biological character. In the course of human experience psychophysical processes may develop needs and satisfactions more

properly designated as psychological, or even sociological;
but the same features will mark the value process at every
level of interest. It is the satisfactions occurring in human
experience, and understood upon reflection as resulting
from specific conditions constituted by deliberate activity
intelligently initiated and promoted, which produce the
values of living. That intelligence is intrinsically and
practically involved in their improvement, enhancement,
and distribution is of pertinent significance to the argument
of this whole discussion.

The consensus of all human judgment would seem to
agree that social relationships constitute the primary
source of highest human values. This is the unequivocal
testimony of the average man as reflected in the high
regard given by common consent to such words in daily
parlance as refer to intimate personal affairs: e. g., home,
husband, wife, son, daughter, father, mother, friend, coun-
try, God, etc. Human history corroborates this judgment in
the record of deeds of heroism and bravery performed at
any cost by those who undertake to guard and to maintain conditions which make such relationships possible.
Supreme honor is readily accorded in the consensus of
universal esteem to those whose conduct has notably indicated their resolution and purpose to preserve and protect
such relationships. The judgment of man on this matter of
personal values cannot be stated in better form than in
this utterance of antiquity: "Greater love hath no man than
this, that a man lay down his life for his friend."

With this agree the findings of the most objective research
into human affairs by the sophisticated techniques of
social science. Both psychology and sociology have long
since concluded that man is primarily and preeminently a
social being. Not only does human nature require social
conditions for its origin and existence, but human welfare

and happiness are so intrinsically grounded in social relationships that human values are actually achieved only in social affairs. Recent discoveries in the psychology of personality point directly to the significance of stability and equanimity of social environment in the development and maintenance of personality and character. Sociology has noted the destructive impact of social calamity upon both morals and morale of unfortunate victims of hopeless disaster. The alarming increase in the incidence of personality disintegration in urban life where face-to-face personal relationships are difficult to establish and often impossible to maintain has made psychiatric service a recognized community responsibility. Here again the conclusions of the most technical examinations concur in the truth of that ancient insight: "it is not good for man to be alone."

It belongs to the character of the most widely held system of religious beliefs in America to be formulated in terms of personal relationships. God is conceived to be a person; faith in God is set forth as a matter of personal trust in Him; the benefits of His favor and help are described as personal satisfaction, assurance, joy, gladness, etc.; the relationship of God to His worshippers is indicated in the designation of "Father"; men are invited to become His "children"; and destiny is conceived in the form of a Heavenly home. Worship is promoted as the adoration of a personal Being; praise is offered to one who hears; prayer is addressed to One who cares; and petition is made to One who can answer. The most awful punishment is conceived to be that of being banished, "excommunicated," to the fate of Cain—a homeless wanderer; the greatest joy is to be reconciled in "atonement," in "the bosom of Abraham," to enjoy the felicity of unbroken communion in love. This personal language prevails throughout the recorded utterances of the Founder of the Christian religion: His appeal to men is thus stated, "Come unto me all ye that are weary and heavy laden, and I will give you rest." His promises are tender in personal interest: "I will not leave you to be orphans; I will come to you." The testimony of all religious biography is eloquent in revealing the personal character of the devotion of the saints. There can be no doubt that when Christian beliefs are set forth in impersonal terms the historic character of this religious system is obscured if not destroyed; and certainly both its appeal and its practical significance are greatly reduced and delimited.

It remains to be noted that the empirical basis of Dewey's philosophical system supports his ready acceptance of the common judgment of all men as to the preeminent importance of social conditions for the weal or woe of mankind. There is no hesitation on his part to hold humane issues as having proper priority over all else in nature. At the same time, his view of man in nature, and his confidence in experimental inquiry as being nature's own procedure of achieving the highest possible ends, lead him directly to the conviction that scientific methods could and should be employed in the realization of life's most cherished treasures. That such is not now being done, to the detriment of man's own interests, is the opinion which Dewey has recently expressed in these words:

Under present conditions scientific methods take effect in determining the concrete economic conditions under which the mass of men live. But they are not employed to determine freely and systematically the moral, the humane, ends served by engrossing practical conditions, the actual state of ends and values. Hence the more important things are left to decision by custom, prejudice, class interests, and traditions embodied in institutions,

whose results are mostly fixed by the superior power in possession of those who manage them.[103]

The ground for holding that the very best procedures
known at this time should be applied in handling such
matters lies in the supreme importance of what is at stake.

There are issues in the conduct of human affairs in their production of good and evil which, at a given time and place, are
so central, so strategic in position, that their urgency deserves
with respect to practice, the names ultimate and comprehensive.
These issues demand the most systematic reflective attention
that can be given.[104]

Dewey considers that the present situation in human
thought, wherein there is "refusal to employ in social
affairs, in the field of human relations, the methods . . . that
are matters of course in dealing with physical things, and
to which we owe the conquest of physical nature," provides for the dominance of the physical in the lives of men.

Our failure to use in matters of direct human concern the
scientific methods which have revolutionized physical knowledge
has permitted the latter to dominate the social scene.[105]

The inference seems plain that such conditions are not
conducive to the achieving of the highest and greatest
potential benefits. Dewey's great confidence in education as
a means of advancing the fortunes and welfare of men
moves him to seek its most effectual promotion; and for
this he considers scientific procedures most eminently
suited. However, the nature of man being what it is, he
feels that for all the efficiency of science there will be no
satisfying results unless and until these methods are extended to deal with social, personal, human affairs. Thus he
points out:

Scientific method and conclusions will not have gained a fundamentally important place in education until they are seen and

treated as supreme agencies in giving direction to collective and cooperative human behavior.[106]

The immediate context of these passages is pointed toward the need for improving man's treatment of human problems on a wide scale in society, but it is probably quite legitimate in the light of the nature of man and the meaning of religion to note that when Dewey is arguing for an application of experimental thinking in national and international "social" affairs, he is actually waging the fight to open the way to extend this technique into all that is meant by "religion." However, it is not necessary to pitch the consideration of such possible extension in problems arising out of data that are taken from advanced, or sophisticated, "religious" situations. The more basic generalizations that may help to project such application of experimental intelligence into the issue of the realization of religious values will best be formulated in the analysis and interpretation of that aspect of religious experience that is most clearly seen to be human, social, and natural in character.

The immediate aim of this part of this discussion is to note what understanding of the processes of the realization of religious values is afforded by the insights into religious experience which are provided in Dewey's exposition of the operation of experimental intelligence. Inasmuch as religious affairs are human affairs, there would seem to be no difficulty in employing the discoveries already made, of characteristic human processes in other fields and on other levels, to achieve the best possible understanding of events that are distinctively religious. Dewey himself followed such procedure in the matter of "vital phenomena" without qualm, inasmuch as he felt it to be fundamentally sound.

If organic life denotes a phase in history in which natural affairs have reached a point in which characteristic new properties appear, and new ways of acting are released because of

integration of fields hitherto unlinked, there does not seem to be anything extraordinary in the fact that what is known about the earlier "physical" series is applied to interpret and direct vital phenomena; nor in the fact that this application does not exhaust their character nor suffice wholly for their description.[107]

In the course of his analysis of human experience as it manifests different aspects and levels of phenomena with varying degrees of significance for human welfare and happiness, Dewey found that

In general, three plateaux of such fields may be discriminated. The first . . . is physical . . . the second level is that of life . . . the third plateau is that of association, communication, participation. This is still further diversified, consisting of individualities. It is marked throughout its diversities, however, by common properties, which define mind as intellect; possession of and response to meanings.[108]

Obviously these several levels provide for an hierarchy of values in ascending importance, so that while the intrinsic unity of individual experience may involve all three levels in any single concrete event, the greater values will naturally occur on the "higher" planes of "wider" range of potentialities. The "levels" here discriminated would perhaps be adequate to permit description of religious affairs in competent and significant fashion, and yet it is quite credible that Dewey would not object to a fourth plateau upon which even more intimate events, with even more precious enjoyments, may occur. "They twain shall become one" points to something more engrossing, more demanding, more rewarding, more wonderful, than "association." Psychology has classified behavior similar to this as "identification." Its power to arouse, to energize, to inspire devotion, loyalty, service in fidelity, in "esprit de corps," in morale, has been recognized and exploited throughout history and bears tribute to its significance as a source of preeminent values. In fact it would be difficult to grasp the relationship indicated by such phrases as "Abide in me, and I in you," upon any lower level. Even though such phenomena are obviously too immediate and mystic to permit direct 'escription, their occurrence in the course of human events, with antecedent and consequent conditions of such external and objective sort as permit observation, recognition, and manipulation, brings them within t_e range of intellectual processes. The utility of such extended discrimination is grounded in the empirical fact that men regard the satisfactions of contemplation and possession as highly if not more highly than the satisfactions of manipulation and achievement; and so, in the analysis of the occurrence of values it may be expected that this further distinction of a level still higher than "that of association, communication, and participation" may result in yet more competent understanding of the processes involved in the having of life's most precious consummations, namely, religious values.

Dewey's own intellectual research has been developed in the study of temporal continuities of experience *between* events to such a degree as quite to ignore structural aspects as these might be reflected *within* events. He found analysis of the temporal to be practical and dynamic, whereas reflection upon the structural would have been contemplative and esthetic. The former is obviously more suited to a scientific frame of mind, and to a pragmatic mood, such as has characterized American life and thought, of which no one has achieved greater distinction nor rendered greater service as an interpreter than John Dewey. But this is not to deny the intellectual integrity and validity of reflective consideration of that which in its very structure occasions delight in being for us just what it is.

CULTURE

The function of culture in the processes of human nature has been anticipated in the discussion above, but a more careful analysis of this phase of human affairs will show the nature and the significance of its operation. Throughout the description of the nature of man, thus far, the singular import of the individual has been steadily noted; and there is a proper sense in which all that is human is found to be based in the manifold of individual experience. But the social relationships obtaining between individuals in all the affairs of society have a formative bearing in the growth and development of individuals, which is determinative in the structuring of personality. No interpretation of man could be adequate which did not recognize and appreciate this cultural origin of individual character. The specific interest of this discussion in the religious experience of man attaches particular importance to the cultural process in human affairs.

The source of culture is lodged in social interaction, but its manifestation is involved in the instrumentalities, the tools, the customs, the institutions, devised by the art of man in the course of living. The problem of the novel puts a premium upon the results of former experience. Such results are preserved and shared through language, which "sustains a containing culture."

Speech is indeed the mother tongue. It is informed with the temperament and the ways of viewing and interpreting life that are characteristic of the culture of a continuing social group.[100]

This is preeminently the case with all forms of art, which condition the "continuity of culture in passage from one civilization to another as well as within the culture" more than "any other one thing." As the culture of any specific group develops, it manifests an organismic autonomy and singularity, which is reflected in its artistic products.

Every culture has its own collective individuality. Like the individuality of the person from whom a work of art issues, this collective individuality leaves its indelible imprint upon the art that is produced.[110]

Not only does culture so function to actualize in creative fashion its own structure of relationships in the art it produces, but through such art products it shares its distinctive character with all who experience that art in a meaningful way.

Nevertheless, when the art of another culture enters into attitudes that determine our experience genuine continuity is effected. Our own experience does not thereby lose its own individuality but it takes unto itself and weds elements that expand its significance. A community and continuity that do not exist physically are created.[111]

The import of this operation in the religious experience of man seems obvious. The impressive history of Christian missions throughout the world with notable success in any and every culture group in the avowed aim to win converts, and to culture them into the Christian Church as participant members in a unique community which claims unbroken continuity from its inception, would seem to be a case in point. Apparently there is no circumstantial limit to the range of this operation, which in turn manifests infinite potentialities.

The art characteristic of a civilization is the means for entering sympathetically into the deepest elements in the experience of remote and foreign civilizations.[112]

Thus the existence and function of any one culture or civilization may endure effectively and vitally for beyond the boundaries or the life span of any group or generation. Dewey has interpreted this significant role of art in the

preservation and perpetuation of culture with brilliant insight.

There are transient and there are enduring elements in a civilization. The enduring forces are not separate; they are functions of a multitude of passing incidents as the latter are organized into the meanings that form minds. Art is the great force in effecting this consolidation. The individuals who have minds pass away one by one. The work in which meanings have received objective expression endure. They become part of the environment and interaction with this phase of the environment is the axis of continuity in the life of civilization.[113]

Such is the explanation of the phenomena of persistence in specific cultures: a fact of special significance in any interpretation of the problem of education in religion. When any religion is taken to be a form of culture, an understanding of the operations involved in its propagation and perpetuation is gained from an analysis of cultural processes operating throughout human experience.

But an even more profound aspect of the communication of culture through art objects is found in the determinative effects which occur in the individuals involved, who "are what they are in the content of their experience because of the cultures in which they participate." Apparently this function of culture is of no casual or incidental import, but is to be held as basic and essential in the welfare and fortunes of men. Dewey has pointed out that any human being "would be poorer than a beast of the fields were it not for traditions that become a part of his mind, and for institutions that penetrate below his outward actions into his purposes and satisfactions." When it is remembered that both "traditions" and "institutions" are public affairs, the possibilities for the operation of intelligence in the production of character are again notable.

The degree of civilization or sophistication seems to

have no bearing upon the validity of this relation between culture and character.

Neither the savage nor the civilized man is what he is by native constitution but by the culture in which he participates.[114]

Likewise the character of intellectual preoccupation does not alter its significance since "the scientific inquirer, the philosopher, the technologist, also derive their substance from the stream of culture." There seems to be no room for doubt that this principle obtains in religious experience in just this universal way, but Dewey's analysis is carried even more closely to religious problems by his exposition of the development of individual ability and character.

Because "meanings acquired in connection with the use of tools and language exercise a profound influence upon organic feelings," it follows that "the subconscious of a civilized adult reflects . . . all the organic modifications he has undergone." Dewey notes this principle in terms of "tradition" and "power."

For each great tradition is itself an organized habit of vision and of methods of ordering and conveying material. As this habit enters into native temperament and constitution it becomes an essential ingredient of the mind of an artist. Peculiar sensitiveness to certain aspects of nature is thereby developed into a power.[115]

But, as noted above, he would by no means limit its application to art, since he feels "dependence upon tradition" is "an essential factor in original vision and creative expression" in any line of intellectual endeavor. The particular interest in this discussion warrants attention to Dewey's more specific remarks pertaining to the moral character of man as being dependent upon the "collective art of a time," that is, upon the "culture:"

The moral office and human function of art can be intelligently

discussed only in the context of culture. A particular work of
art may have a definite effect upon a particular person or upon
a number of persons . . . . But a less conscious and more massed
constant adjustment of experience proceeds from the total environment that is created by the collective art of a time. Just as
physical life cannot exist without the support of a physical
environment, so moral life cannot go on without the support of
a moral environment.[116]

Dewey has pressed his analysis of this operation in the
cultural process to note its bearing upon the historic
philosophic enigma, "the mind-body problems," and in so
doing has laid bare even more fully its critical significance
in the development of human personality and character,
as the following lengthy excerpt will show:

In a practical sense, here is the heart of the mind-body problem.
Activities which develop, appropriate and enjoy meanings bear
the same actualizing relation to psychophysical affairs as the
latter bear to physical characters. They present the consequences of a wider range of interactions, that in which needs,
efforts and satisfactions conditioned by association are operative,
and in this widened and deepened activity, there are both added
resources and values, and added liabilities and defaults. The
actualization of meanings furnishes psycho-physical qualities
with their ulterior significance and worth. But it also confuses
and perverts them. The effects of this corruption are themselves embodied through habits in the psychophysical, forming
one-sided degraded and excessive susceptibilities; creating both
disassociations and rigid fixations in the sensory register. These
habitual effects become in turn spontaneous, natural, "instinc-
tive"; they form the platform of development and apprehension
of further meanings, affecting every subsequent phase of personal and social life.[117]

That the cultural process in altering, modifying, reconstructing "the native need, adjustment, and satisfaction"
through "the casual growth and incorporation of mean-

ings," so that "psychophysical qualities" are furnished with "their ulterior significance and worth," does make possible "all kinds of aberrations," as Dewey remarks, is obviously undeniable. But it would seem proper to note that it also makes possible the achievement of the values and goods commonly ascribed to civilization. Dewey elaborates his thought in an alarming sketch of bizarre possibilities, which must be admitted as logically sound.

> There then occur systematized withdrawals from intercourse and interaction, from what common sense calls "reality": carefully cultivated and artificially protected fantasies of consolation and compensation; rigidly stereotyped beliefs not submitted to objective tests; habits of learned ignorance or systematized ignorings of concrete relationships; organized fanaticisms; dogmatic traditions which socially are harshly intolerable and which intellectually are institutionalized paranoiac systems: idealizations which instead of being immediate enjoyments of meanings, cut man off from nature and his fellows.

> In short there is constituted what Walter Lippmann has well termed a secondary pseudo-environment, which affects every item of traffic and dealing with the primary environment. Thus the concrete problems of mind-body have their locus and import in the educational procedures by which a normal integration of meanings in organic functions shall be secured and perversions prevented; in the remedial operations of psychiatry, and in social arts and appliances that render intercourse substantial, balanced and flexible.[118]

But to keep a balanced outlook upon the significance of this cultural operation, is it not important to note that the same principle is operative in all the glorious achievements of "civilization" and "refinement"? This question is inserted here somewhat as a demurrer against the impression of a sweeping generalization which would jeopardize the validity of all religious experience. The aptness of much of the phraseology to refer to the common formulations

of religious experience would seem to point such an inference rather patently. That "aberrations" occur in religious experience is notoriously and pathetically true. But that religion and religious values should therefore be summarily dismissed as unfortunate perversions of primary experience need not follow any more than the higher incidence of insanity among civilized people should be accepted as an indictment of social sophistication. The actual working of the cultural process in question is properly seen as morally neutral, being suitable for manipulation and thus a proper situation for the exercise of intelligence. That it can be perverted to result in spurious beliefs and invalid tenets need not be questioned; but that it likewise is involved in the production of genuine "goods" with infinite potentialities of benefit and blessing should certainly be noted. And if it should be once conceded that the nature of man requires that the best shall be preferred, then this particular aspect of the cultural process must be esteemed as being of primary significance. Perhaps one more observation based upon Dewey's analysis of culture should be noted here. There seems to be a dynamic significance in culture not only because of its organic genesis as noted above but even more affectively because of its commemorative character.

Again speaking of the place of ceremonialism in early culture, Goldenweiser well characterizes it as a kind of "psychic" incandescence; because of its presence, there is "no cooling of the ever glowing mass (the conglomerate of customs), no flagging of the emotions, no sinking of the cultural associations to the more precarious level of purely ideational connections." [119]

Such "psychic" response is shared by the novitiate as he enters sympathetically into the past which is being commemorated. The function of language, of speech, has been noted: being "informed with the temperament and the ways

of viewing and interpreting life that are characteristic of
the culture of a continuing social group." "Traditions" have
been remarked to "become a part of his mind," and
"institutions" have been seen to "penetrate below his outward actions into his purposes and satisfactions." Thus,
as a man becomes "cultured" he not only manifests a
certain form and pattern of character but exhibits a characteristic mode of purpose and initiative, derived from his
specific cultural milieu. Thus it is to be held as quite
natural that when an individual participates in a religious
culture, as manifested by any continuing group or society,
he not only acquires the characteristic forms of habit,
attitude, belief, etc., as these are manifested in the course
of his conduct, but he shares the purposes, the disposition,
the will, intrinsic in that culture. No more profound
significance can be conceived in human experience, since
this operation produces the cast of character of man, and
so determines the kind of world he and his fellows shall
live in. When the preeminent character of religious values
and goods is held in mind, the import of the cultural process
is incomparable.

The subtle, indirect, and ofttimes unconscious manner
in which this operation occurs renders the function of
intelligence therein somewhat less obvious. The bearing of
culture upon the formation of character is so covert as to
be quite unconscious. There would seem to be little scope
for the exercise of intelligent reflection and choice as the
specific actions of the individual are formulated. But when
once the general function of culture is recognized, then
the possibility of determining one's own individuality by
the selection of one's cultural habitat in the choice of
associates, companions, friends, becomes apparent, and a
situation develops wherein intelligence can operate effectively. So a man can determine the kind of man he

will be, and thus·the kind of world there shall be, by intelligently committing himself as a participant in the life and culture of a specific social group.

The survey of the description of the nature of man as set forth in this chapter is basically important in the whole discussion being presented. Whatever there may be in religion, it is what man has, and so is to be understood according to his nature. The purpose of this study will be furthered in the noting of some observations by way of pointing pertinent aspects of the description which has been reviewed.

Throughout this whole treatment there has been no attempt to discuss metaphysical matters. Experimentalist conceptions are essentially descriptive of empirical events as these appear objectively. An exhaustive analysis of what may inhere in subjective consciousness does not properly come within the experimentalist perspective inasmuch as that which is unique, ineffable in its character, is not available for the comparison, consensus, and consideration necessary for identification, interpretation, and verification. Accordingly, the whole issue of metaphysical entities characteristically involved in religious beliefs, even the validity of the idea of man's own being, his personal entity, remains outside the scope of the description as given. Dewey simply does not refer to entities which may or may not exist metaphysically. While it is therefore obvious he does not affirm such existences, it may be noted again that he does not deny such. As a matter of approach, Dewey's thought moves on the objective, empirical plane. He describes, analyzes, interprets, studies events, as they occur as seen. Whatever else may be real and even vital is neither here nor there. The elaboration of his study of man is kept in this perspective, and on the plane of his conscious philosophic outlook and interest. He seeks to refrain from what he would esteem fanciful speculation, and with all due regard for the integrity of others, he will admit for consideration only such data as he would consider public, eventual, and actual.

Hence, in his conception of mind, Dewey refers to no existence, no substance, no single "thing" as such. "Mind" is not substance: the word is not properly a "substantive." "Mind" is more "verb" than "noun." "Mind" is being had, it does. "Mind" exists in, apart from, beyond any individual being; but it exists as an event, a system of events, based primarily in the "awareness" which characterizes human experience. "Self" is an organization of relationships, integrated under the influence of a unification process whereby the singularity of the particular organism is being manifested and achieved. "Society" is likewise an organization of communal relationships as these exist in eventual experiences of man. "Beliefs" are structures of commitment. "Values" are satisfactions confirmed by critical judgment. "Culture" is the embodiment of collective experience objects. Such language makes no reference beyond or outside its own conscious perspective. It is designedly "instrumental," and as such has no "final" significance. Whatever merit may or may not inhere in the ideas of men as to their individual beings, their "immortal souls," their "eternal destiny," there are no criteria afforded in this description of human nature that will serve for appraisal of validity of such concepts. This point is being reiterated in order that the discussion of the Meaning of Religion in the next chapter, being set forth in experimentalist terms, will not be charged with any responsibility to deal with metaphysical reality or final verity. It will suffice to keep in mind that man does have religious experience, he does cherish religious values, and he does seek personal goods through religious practices. The actual

status of entities referred to in religious beliefs has no more bearing upon the processes of religion than the actual status of entities employed in physical interpretation has upon the processes of science. This is not meant to imply that metaphysical existences are a matter of indifference but to keep in mind that the approach being taken does not include their reality within its purview. In the experience of mankind one aspect of intellectual interest has been designated as religion, and it is to the meaning of religion in human affairs as it is to be described in the discourse of experimentalism that our thought is now directed.

V: THE MEANING OF RELIGION

The conscious activities of man manifest a threefold differentiation commonly designated as Science, Art, and Religion. Despite infinite variation in conceptualization and wide fluctuation in zeal, the distinctive characters of these three fields of preoccupation make them discriminable for practical purposes; but their interrelationships in actual human experience are so basic that a comprehensive grasp of all is prerequisite to an adequate understanding of each. The primary interest in this discussion is in religion, but to gain a competent idea of the meaning of religion it is necessary to have in mind something of the meaning of science and the meaning of art as well.

Differences in meanings ascribed to constructs produced in these three areas respectively have been so marked and at times so sharp as to suggest fundamental conflict even to the point of basic discontinuity in human consciousness. Thus dualistic ideas of irreconcilable opposition to one another have been inferred with resultant partisanship in devotion. This cleavage has been manifested most dramatically between science and religion, as modern history has witnessed heated controversy between scientists and theologians. An experimental interpretation of empirical data, however, invalidates such assumption of disorganization in the mind of man. Men have exercised themselves in diverse manner in science, art, and religion, and have produced variant results, both good and bad; but they have ever been men and have behaved throughout as men behave. Intellectualization in all aspects of experience manifests a consistent pattern. The comprehension of

underlying continuity does not appear in reconciliation of sophisticated conclusions reached in the several fields but in the organic unity of the individual involved.

As a matter of fact, apparent conflict between ideas held in these different areas need not be too highly regarded. Difference of opinion is a well-known trait of human thought, and such difference occurs not only between the three major fields indicated but also within each. Scientists do not differ only with religionists: they differ, and often quite sharply, with scientists. The acceptance of common premises tends to reduce contention, but it would seem that no area of human concern may escape its blessings or its curse. Yet harmony both has been empirically manifested and is logically demonstrable. The notion that science, art, and religion are practical alternatives is sound only in the limited sense of personal interest or loyalty. There seems to be no intrinsic necessity for such disparateness.

The point of departure for an understanding of the unity existing throughout the multiform activities and the manifold consciousness of man is a recognition of the biological singularity of the individual organism and the potential multiplicity of his total environment which results in variant interests vying for his attention. The situation is complicated by the shifting focus of his own needs in the course of his life span. Persistent attention to the man as such, as the unit of human affairs, will serve to reveal that the "opacity of bias" which operates to distinguish the individual also functions to integrate his multiverse interests and activities with unifying effect. He is the one who considers to manipulate his environment, contrives to communicate his experience to others, and contemplates his status and character in terms of eventual destiny. That these axes of personal interest should develop mutually distinctive forms of thought is easily expected. The remarkable thing is that they can ever be integrated. The fact is that such integration is feasible only within the life experience of the individual. From that point of view an understanding of their several distinctive characters is logically possible without being diverted into any schematic disunity.

SCIENCE

The biological situation involves man in organic relations with his environment in which his vital needs are satisfied through adjustive selection. Mental capacity enables him to be aware of meanings and to know objects, infinitely increasing the scope of possibilities for successful manipulation in his affairs. Recognition of the role of environment in the achievement of satisfactions or "goods" generates interest in, and guides the solution of, the problem of control with the aim of securing preferred "goods" at pleasure. This interest is original in the development of science.

The distinctively intellectual attitude which marks scientific inquiry was generated in efforts at controlling persons and things so that consequences, issues, outcomes would be more stable and assured.[1]

But such interest is not limited distinctively to the project of science. It appears as a function of the traits of natural existence, and as such it generates superstitious magic as well as rational science. Both these modes of procedure are inspired by the desire to secure results through manipulation, and are to be distinguished only by the relative merits of their characteristic methods.

The traits of natural existence which generate the fears and adorations of superstitious barbarians generate the scientific procedure of disciplined civilization. The superiority of the

latter does not consist in the fact that they are based on "real" existence, while the former depend wholly upon a human nature different from nature in general. It consists in the fact that scientific inquiries reach *objects* which are better, because reached by method which controls them, and which adds greater control to life itself, method which mitigates accident, turns contingency to account, and releases thought and other forms of endeavor.[2]

Dewey has remarked the significant trait of magic to be its indifference to causal relationships embodied in means: a condition that minimizes intelligence as a factor in its operations.

The principle of magic is found whenever it is hoped to get results without intelligent control of means; and also when it is supposed that means can exist and yet remain inert and inoperative.[3]

That this character of magic may be observed in much religious practice cannot and need not be denied, but it is held to be equally true that the intelligent technique of science is as applicable in the effort to achieve and distribute moral and spiritual goods as it has been so notably demonstrated in the material realm.

The distinctive character of science is a function of a basic intellectual conception of nature, in which it is held that an underlying continuity of causal relationships persists throughout all concrete events.[4] The existence of unique temporal immediate qualities is not denied; but the regular permanent general traits which constitute the order of causal sequence are sought to provide the knowledge upon which understanding and control can be based. This approach of science, designed to arrive at instrumental knowledge and mechanisms of control, employs a fundamental technique of abstraction, which facilitates practical results but marks such as valid only within the specific limitations of the purpose in hand. Dewey has noted in historical comment that "science and invention did not get on" until "the mind turned squarely around" from its preoccupation with "special forces to account for," and men "set about breaking up phenomena into minute detail and searching for correlations." It may be remarked that such outlook and approach remain prerequisite in scientific procedure. The practical benefits of this technique are conceived as sufficient warrant for the immediate loss of qualitative aspects in the artificial objectifying involved. That such loss occurs is readily admitted; but it would be a gratuitous fallacy to assume that immediate qualities have thereby been eliminated from experience or significance. Dewey states plainly that "the surrender of immediate qualities, sensory and significant, as objects of science" did not alter the constitution of reality, but rather that such intellectual tactics "left in reality these immediate qualities just as they were." Far from implying that such procedure intimates any lack of importance, Dewey points out:

And also without immediate qualities those relations with which science deals, would have no footing in existence, and thought would have nothing beyond itself to chew upon or dig into.[5]

Were this intellectual character of science more commonly understood, much tension which now exists because of the fear that science repudiates existential status of objects cherished in beliefs and enshrined in values would be avoided. Dewey notes the historic occurrence of this apprehension:

Multiplied and secure ends depend upon letting go existent ends, reducing them to indicative and implying means. The great historic obstacle to science was unwillingness to make the surrender, lest moral, esthetic, and religious objects suffer.[6]

He goes on to point out that no such damage need follow:

Reduction of natural existences to the status of means thus presents nothing inherently adverse to possessed and appreciated ends, but rather renders the latter a more secure and extensive affair.[7]

It belongs to the cultural prestige which science has attained in its impressive record of achievement that the mind of man tends to ascribe superiority in terms of reality to its conceptions and conclusions. But no one could be more definite than Dewey in decrying such mistaking the significance of scientific thinking. He has noted that

For purposes except that of general and extensive translation of one conception into another, it does not follow that the "scientific" way is the best way of thinking an affair.[8]

Dewey goes on to brand this an almost inexcusable error:

There is something both ridiculous and disconcerting in the way in which men have let themselves be imposed upon, so as to infer that scientific ways of thinking of objects give the inner reality of things, and that they put a mark of spuriousness upon all other ways of thinking of them, and of perceiving and enjoying them. It is ludicrous because these scientific conceptions, like other instruments, are hand-made by man in pursuit of realization of a certain interest—that of the maximum convertibility of every object of thought into any and every other.[9]

Yet the legend of general superiority in validity and importance of scientific ideas is so impressive and so persistent in popular thinking, especially when compared with moral and religious conceptions, that the elaboration of this exposition by an even more close analysis of the procedure of science to discover the basis of its actual significance seems important.

Homogeneity is the quality in scientific objects which

facilitates inference and constitutes the infinite scope of significance in the potentialities of application which makes science so preeminently useful in practical affairs. Its importance can scarcely be overestimated *for the purposes of science,* but it is to be noted that this quality inheres primarily in the method and then appears artificially in the abstractions produced by scientific processes. The significance of this observation is felt when it is seen that heterogeneity marks natural affairs: a condition that is deliberately ignored in the scientific approach.

Physical science disregards the qualitative heterogeneity of experienced objects so as to make them all members of one comprehensive homogeneous scheme, and hence capable of translation or conversion one into another.[10]

Thus the homogeneity of science is apparently derived not as a reflection of some basic trait in Nature but from the quantitative results of metric operational procedures; and the translatability so highly prized appears to be a function of the mathematics involved. This observation is corroborated by such a comment as follows concerning the nature of science objects:

The net effect of modern inquiry makes it clear that these constancies, whether the larger ones termed laws or the lesser ones termed facts, are statistical in nature. They are the products of averaging large numbers of observed frequencies by means of a series of operations. They are not descriptions of the exact structure and behavior of any *individual* thing, any more than the actuarial "law" of the frequency of deaths of persons having a certain age is an account of the life of one of the persons included in the calculation.[11]

So it would appear that the validity of the resultant "objects" is logically confined to the uses of science, and any attempt to conceive the essence, the intrinsic nature, of "events" or "things" from such scientific conclusions would

involve bald hypostasy. As long as the data being handled concern inanimate matter, this limitation can scarcely be felt; in dealing with animals limited to "instinct" it will not be important en masse; but in dealing with man it is notoriously inadequate from the standpoint of his personal interests and for purposes of living.

Heterogeneity in common sense, on the other hand, is a function of the differentiation of the senses, a trait of the manifold of consciousness; and as such is the ground for the rich possibilities of precious treasures, cherished values, etc., which distinguish human experience. However practical it may be to disregard this heterogeneity in concrete affairs while pursuing the purposes of science, it would seem to be a gross error to suspend reflection upon human affairs when the abstract conclusions of science have been formulated, as if such were to be accorded final significance. Doubtless there is a special sense in which scientific results do have final qualities but this is not the general over-all humane sense in which philosophic reflection is to be worthily pursued. Dewey says:

Intellectual meanings may themselves be appropriated, enjoyed and appreciated; but the character of intellectual meaning is instrumental.[12]

In fact, the instrumental character of intellectual material is so definitive that Dewey holds "science" to be "properly a handmaiden that conducts natural events" to the "happy issue" of "immediately enjoyed possession." At one point he writes:

We are here concerned to emphasize the fact that elimination of the qualities of experienced existence is merely an intermediate step necessary to the discovery of relations, and that when it is accomplished the scientific object becomes the means of control of occurrence of experienced things having a richer and more secure enjoyment of values and qualities.[13]

But in even more sweeping fashion he summarizes the whole point being stressed here in this succinct statement:

It is congenial to our idiom to call the reflective conclusions of competent methods by the name of science. But science thus conceived is not a final thing. The final thing is appreciation and use of things of direct experience. These are *known* in as far as their constitutents and their form are the result of science. They are natural objects experienced in relations and continuities that are summed up in rich and definite individual forms.[14]

The actual significance of science in the attainment and administration of the highest goods is not impaired or diminished by this recognition of its instrumental character. On the contrary, the natural constitution of human experience points the potential function of science and grounds its practical import. It is true that Dewey freely recognizes that

No mechanically exact science of an individual is possible. An individual is a history unique in character.[15]

But this very fact, that human affairs are histories, indicates the existence of regular tangible mechanical elements in the form of organic environmental conditions, involved in the course of what happens. Here science can operate with practical significance.

In explicit discovery of just the conditions antecedent to this good and that bad, it puts in our hands means of regulating the occurrence of things possessed of these qualities.[16]

Though the method of science was developed in the study of physical data, there would seem to be no limit to the range of its applicability. It is of special interest for this discussion to note that Dewey sees no hindrance in the nature of all that is involved to the project of utilizing scientific method in the administration and improvement of all human values, including the religious.

What is there to exclude a belief that science, while it has grasp of the regular and stable mechanism of nature, is also an organ of regulating and enriching, through its own expansion, the more exuberant and irregular expressions of nature in human intercourse, the arts, religions, industry and politics?"

The actual pattern of scientific technique wherever employed needs little elaboration here. It will suffice to note that the primary phase is one of search for the mechanical order of sequential relations involved in the occurrence of whatever is being studied. Attention is focused upon the way in which events occur, and so prepares the situation for deliberate manipulation. Scientific reflection and thinking produces knowledge objects as "an order of relations which serve as tools to effect immediate havings and beings."

The character of the object is like that of a tool, say a lever; it is an order of determination of sequential changes terminating in a foreseen consequence.[18]

Thus science "adds to the casual having of ends an ability to regulate the date, place and manner of their emergence."

The empirical integrity as well as the humanistic quality of Dewey's thought is indicated in his pressing the secondary phase of science, controlled direction of events, as an intrinsic aspect essential to the whole project. There is no proper status for a truncated "science" which seeks only to "know."

What is sometimes termed "applied" science, may then be more truly science than is what is conventionally called pure science, for it is directly concerned with not just instrumentalities, but instrumentalities at work in effecting modifications of existence in behalf of conclusions that are reflectively preferred.[19]

Dewey expresses this idea in categoric fashion when he writes:

Only as science is seen to be fulfilled and brought to itself in intelligent management of historical processes in their continuity can man be envisaged as within nature, and not as a supernatural extrapolation. Just because nature is what it is, history is capable of being more truly known—understood, intellectually realized—than are mathematics and physical objects. . . . While the humanizing of science contributes to the life of humanity, it is even more required in behalf of science, in order that it may be intelligible, simple and clear; in order that it may have that correspondence with reality which true knowledge claims for itself.[20]

The ground for the argument involved seems to lie in the requirements of philosophical validity and integrity, so that Dewey can scarcely be charged with ulterior moral or ethical motives when he asserts dogmatically:

The genuine interests of "pure" science are served only by broadening the idea of application to include all phases of liberation and enrichment of human experience.[21]

But more than dialectic integrity is at stake at this point. A clue to understanding the tragic prostitution of scientific methods to the service of inhuman and antisocial ends, such as has marked world history in our time, is implied in this insight into the importance of integrating external scientific procedures with the deeper inner intangibles: character and purpose:

As long as our own fundamental psycho-physical attitudes in dealing with external things are subconscious, our conscious attention going only to the relations of external things, so long will our perception of the external situations be subject at its root to perversion and vitiation.[22]

The critical import of such integration which would direct the operations of science in the service of man's highest values has been indicated above, but it is to be noted that for this development science in itself, while

eminently useful, is not competent. Fortunately for man, science is not the only nor even the most significant aspect of human consciousness. It should be remembered that to take science in any unilateral sense is to project a violent and dangerous disorganization into human affairs. There is a basic unity in the human individual which keeps science functioning in harmonious collaboration in the whole of human activity. This thought has been carefully developed by Dewey, who has remarked that while "philosophy has often entertained the ideal of complete integration of knowledge," such a possibility does not exist. In so far as we hold science to be the source of our knowing, "knowledge by its nature is analytic and discriminating." The normal course of scientific inquiry "defeats the idea of any complete synthesis of knowledge upon an intellectual basis." Dewey's summary of this matter points definitely to something else than science needed to realize the potential benefits possible through scientific procedures:

Nevertheless the need for integration of specialized results of science remains, and philosophy should contribute to the satisfaction of the need.

The need, however, is practical and human rather than intrinsic to science itself; the latter is content as long as it can move to new problems and discoveries. The need for direction of action in large social fields is the source of a genuine demand for unification of scientific conclusions. They are organized when their bearing on the conduct of life is disclosed.[33]

That such "bearing on the conduct of life" is involved in the meaning of Religion will be set out below.

ART

The course of human experience in organic environmental interactions appears as a continuum of sequential events and affairs causally interrelated with all that is in the universe. This stream of history is marked by moments of satisfaction and fulfillment possessing immediate traits of esthetic quality. It is possible that the precarious character of biological existence grounds the sense of joy and exuberance in satisfactions of triumph and success as these occur.

For only when an organism shares in the ordered relations of its environment does it secure the stability essential to living. And when the participation comes after a phase of disruption and conflict, it bears within itself the germs of a consummation akin to the esthetic.[24]

Whatever the genetic conditions may be, esthetic experience highlights the common life of all men, imparting significance, facilitating intelligence, and generating values, so that activity becomes meaningful and worth while. Such pin points of consummation guide the interest and direct the purpose of conscious effort.

For man is more preoccupied with enhancing life than with bare living; so that a sense of living when it attends labor and utility is borrowed not intrinsic, having been generated in those periods of relief when activity was dramatic.[25]

Certainly as they are "had" they are "prized," and their recurrence is sought after.

Esthetic experience is constituted by "immediately felt relations of order and fulfillment" which occur because nature manifests "ordered variation of changes" appearing as "rhythm" or "symmetry" according to perceptual conditions, and appears to be indigenous in human affairs.

There are situations in which self-enclosed, discrete, individualized characters dominate. They constitute the subject matter of esthetic experience; and every experience is esthetic in as far as it is final or arouses no search for some other experience.

When this complete quality is conspicuous the experience is denominated esthetic.[26]

That the esthetic should qualify fine art may be taken as a matter of course, but that it is involved in practical and in intellectual affairs is a fact that warrants special notice. Dewey has pointed out:

Even the utility of things, their capacity to be employed as means and agencies, is first of all not a relation, but a quality possessed; immediately possessed, it is as esthetic as any other quality. If labor transforms an orderly sequence into a means of attaining ends, this not only converts a casual ending into a fulfillment, but it also gives labor an immediate quality of finality and consummation.[27]

Since "labor" is by no means limited to the manual variety, the observation just quoted is to be held as valid for all thinking.

When there is genuine artistry in scientific inquiry and philosophic speculation, a thinker proceeds neither by rule nor yet blindly, but by means of meanings that exist immediately as feelings having qualitative color.[28]

It is this sense of completeness, of fulfillment, of satisfaction in success which identifies the right answer, the proper attitude, the suitable act in every problematic situation. While Dewey recognizes "a difference between the esthetic and the intellectual" as a matter of accent, he holds "the ultimate matter of both emphases in experience is the same." The integral unity of human consciousness is thus maintained and a basis is recognized for the fact that esthetic quality is essential to the integrity of all experience.

The undefined pervasive quality of an experience is that which binds together all the defined elements, the objects of which we are focally aware, making them a whole.[29]

This very fact, that esthetic quality, "the unity of experience," is intrinsically and necessarily involved in all experience, points directly to its presence in religious affairs, and so makes an understanding of its function pertinent, if not prerequisite, to an understanding of the meaning of religion.

While esthetic quality may thus be viewed in abstraction and noted as immediate, unique, spontaneous in character, and as such ineffable, inscrutable, unpredictable, and unmanageable, it never occurs actually in isolation. Though distinctive, it is never disparate. Final and instrumental qualities inhere in identical concrete affairs. It is the occurrence of the unique in conjunction with the regular that was seen to facilitate scientific procedure in controlling the having of immediate experiences. Likewise it is the presence of the regular in rhythmic order that supplies the form which can be perceived as characterizing the occurrence of esthetic experiences. Dewey hald it to be a mistake to conceive "form" or "structure" as anything more existential than an arrangement, an order of relations, which in art are to be taken as "modes of interaction." The instrumental nature of his thought is plainly in view when he points out:

Order, for esthetic purposes, is defined and measured by functional and operative traits.[30]

Apparently the "order" which is an intrinsic element in any "percept" is not as such actually "out there." Dewey holds that perception is more than recognition since it actually involved an exercise of energy "to *take* in" what is being perceived. Thus in perception it follows that "a beholder must *create* his own experience." Such creativity, however, produces results that are additive rather than original.

"Art" does not create the forms; it is their selection and organi-

zation in such ways as to enhance, prolong and purify the perceptual experience."[31]

"Form" represents "what is involved in the organization of space and time prefigured in every course of a developing life-experience," and thus is seen to be "a character of every experience that is *an* experience," being necessary for its realization.

Form may then be defined as the operation of forces that carry the experience of an event, object, scene, and situation to its own integral fulfillment.[32]

The perception of form in which the beholder lays hold upon regular elements in the consummatory event to conceive the conditions which will induce, sustain, and enhance experience of esthetic quality is the incipient phase of the operation of art.

The characteristic interest of man to seek the prolongation, enhancement, and recurrence of consummatory experience inspires him to express his perception in some objective formulation of suitable material that will serve as a functional medium for his purpose. At this point intelligence is exercised.

An incredible amount of observation and of the kind of intelligence that is exercised in perception of qualitative relations characterizes creative work in art.[33]

The creative aspect appears as a function of the individual who is remaking the world as he sees it.

The *material* out of which a work of art is composed belongs to the common world rather than to the self, and yet there is self-expression in art because the self assimilates the material in a distinctive way to reissue it into the public world in a form that builds a new object.[34]

This productive phase of the operation of art, the artistic, achieves expression by "reducing the raw material" of any experience "to matter ordered through form." The resultant art product is actually a transformation of nature into meaningful objects.

What makes a material a medium is that it is used to express a meaning which is other than that which it is in virtue of its bare physical existence: the meaning not of what it physically is, but of what it expresses.[35]

Thus the actual significance of religious objects is not to be appraised by the reductive analyses of interpretative techniques developed in social science theory. Religion will involve activities which in themselves may be taken psychophysically to mean one thing, but when employed as media of expression must be held as meaning something else: in fine, what they were intended to express. The criterion of their expressive efficiency in the philosophy of John Dewey would be the same for religious products as for any other kind.

The common element in all the arts, technological and useful, is an organization of energy as means for producing a result.[36]

Both esthetic and artistic aspects are manifested in art products. However, the multiple characters which may be abstractly noted in analytic survey do not exist as conglomerate, but are manifested in monolithic unity in art as experience.

In art as an experience, actuality and possibility or ideality, the new and the old, objective material and personal response, the individual and the universal, surface and depth, sense and meaning, are integrated in an experience in which they are all transfigured from the significance that belongs to them when isolated in reflection.[37]

Apparently such integration is the result of a process blending variegated aspects of life and environment, infusing relations with emotions in the immediate experience

of man. Not only does the art process produce a single unitary experience manifesting unique form, but such result possesses a final and absolute character that resists alteration or modification. Dewey has remarked:

Of any artistic act or product it may be said both that it is inevitable in its rightness, that nothing in it can be altered without altering all, and that its occurrence is spontaneous, unexpected, fresh, unpredictable.[38]

Thus it would appear that in a world which has been noted as one of constant and interminable change, there are produced in the course of the history of man objective forms at once complete and permanent as a result of art. Something of the uniqueness of the individual in his spontaneity is incorporated in the art products in which he manifests, records, and celebrates "the life of a civilization."

At any one fell moment when the individual experiences consummatory satisfaction there is finality and completeness, which are unique, real, and precious. The perception of the form of that experience is likewise complete. It is what it is, then and there, and for him. When his effort to express himself is successful he produces an object with balance, proportion, symmetry, and fitness that is again final, leaving no desire for further effort. And when that object "affords continuously renewed delight," so that it is "indefinitely instrumental to *new* satisfying events," it exhibits "universal" character in its meaning.

The "eternal" quality of great art is its renewed instrumentality for further consummatory experiences.[39]

This consideration of the nature of art products affords an insight into one phase of religious experience which has been seriously questioned from the scientific point of view. The fact that "art" arises in "final" experience so that products of art are "complete" and "unmodifiable" in their symmetry, their rhythm, so that any alteration amounts to a destruction, provides ground for understanding a stubborn insistence in historic "expressions" of religious faith in affirming an unalterable finality. If such expressions stood as statistical judgments or summary conclusions, the ongo of events would require their enlargement, alteration, correction, and modification; but if such expressions appear in history as "artistic" products embodying the "esthetic" form of completed experience, as "art products," they must be allowed to stand as final. Whether they are to be accepted as valid is a matter of their instrumental efficacy, to be tested in pragmatic fashion. Their acceptability is a matter of the more basic interest of the individual. Their art quality is indicated by their suitability to induce, sustain, and enhance the particular experience out of which they were formulated. Such would seem to be the origin and nature of classic "symbols" as employed in promotion of religious affairs.

While art is primarily a matter of esthetic appreciation and artistic expression, the products of art have a broad instrumental significance in the affairs of men. As man perceives that his satisfactions occur under certain conditions,

He begins to manage and order his activities in reference to their consequences. The consequences undergone because of doing are incorporated as the means of subsequent doings because the relation between doing and undergoing is perceived."[40]

This is doubtless a phase of the knowledge process, but it is also the operation of art.

For all the intelligent activities of men, no matter whether expressed in science, fine arts, or social relationships, have for their task the conversion of causal bonds, relations of succession,

into a connection of means-consequence, into meanings. When the task is achieved the result is art: and in art everything is common between means and ends."[41]

These products are the tools, the instrumentalities, by which practical operations are facilitated and instrumental meanings are incorporated into mechanisms of control. Thus "immediate experience" is enriched through "control over action" in an additive way, since "possibilities are embodied in works of art that are not elsewhere actualized."

Art is a continuation, by means of intelligent selection and arrangement, of natural tendencies of natural events. . . . Either art is a continuation, by means of intelligent selection and arrangement, of natural tendencies of natural events, or art is a peculiar addition to nature springing from something dwelling exclusively within the breast of man, whatever name be given the latter. In the former case, delightfully enhanced perception or esthetic appreciation is of the same nature as enjoyment of any object that is consummatory. It is the outcome of a skilled and intelligent art of dealing with natural things for the sake of intensifying, purifying, prolonging and deepening the satisfactions which they spontaneously afford. That, in this process, new meanings develop, and that these afford uniqely new traits and modes of enjoyment is but what happens everywhere in emergent growths."[42]

Dewey considers such products of art to be "nature transformed by entering into new relationships." While he holds that "in no case can a work of art rival the infinite concreteness of nature," he seems to accord the results of the art process at least equal if not superior status in their import to man.

The goods of art are not less good in their goodness than the gifts of nature, while in addition they are such as to bring with themselves open-eyed confidence. They are the fruit of means consciously employed, fulfillments whose further consequences are secured by conscious control of the causal conditions which enter into them."

As this instrumental character of art is considered, the distinction between science and art as different modes of activity tends to fade away. Far from being separate they appear interwoven in the processes of nature, where "art" is to be seen as "the complete culmination of nature," and "science" is held to be "properly a handmaiden that conducts natural events to this happy issue." Dewey admits that this auxiliary role of science is not yet recognized in current thought, but he esteems "the power of art" to be relatively so great that

Science itself is but a central art auxiliary to the generation and utilization of other arts."

In his elaboration of his analysis in *Art as Experience,* Dewey has traced out such aspects of the mutual interrelationships between art and science, but has not undertaken a similar exposition of relationships involving religion. That such relationships do exist, that they are natural, and as such are intelligible in much the same fashion as those which have been considered, would seem to stand without question. An approach to such exposition will be sketched in the subsequent section of this chapter.

The function of art through the instrumental character of its products is thus seen to be considerable and general throughout all the processes of human nature, but there is a particular sense in which its significance is especially important to the life experience of the individual. Art products, being "expressive of a deep seated attitude of adjustment, of an underlying idea and ideal of generic human attitude," are the means which make it possible for an individual to enter "sympathetically into the deepest elements in the experience of remote and foreign civiliza-

tions." In the case of religious experience this is particularly vital bcause of the effect upon formal intellectual material.

But because of the esthetic strand, religious teachings were the more readily conveyed and their effect was the more lasting. By the art in them, they were changed from doctrines into living experiences.[45]

Dewey has remarked:

Possibilities are embodied in works of art that are not elsewhere actualized.[46]

There would seem to be no definite limit which can be assigned to the dynamic sweep of such possibilities:

Impulsion beyond all limits that are externally set inheres in the very nature of the artist's work.[47]

These observations seem to provide a basis for explaining the impressive power of religious art, manifested as it is in the multiform means employed to promote and propagate religious experience. Such instrumentalities may appear as rites, ceremonies, songs, creeds, sermons, sacraments, programs, literature, etc., transformed by their esthetic quality and art character into means for inducing experiences had by those who have produced them: experiences that may be other and more than any had by the individual himself. Such bearing is implied when Dewey observes:

Art has been the means of keeping alive the sense of purposes that outrun evidence, and of meanings that transcend indurated habit.[40]

Certainly there reed be no further search for other means that will enable the individual to enter into other experiences, even other civilizations, other cultures, than such as he could expect in his own natural environment. The works of art not only facilitate a lateral diffusion of culture apart from the prerequisite of identical generic histories,

but they enable the individual to enter into the very
experience of others "remote" and "foreign" from his own
circumstances. When it is recalled that mind is constituted
as a structure of meanings and that meanings are embodied
in products of art, the intimate practical relation between
art and mental activity is readily seen. Since art incorporates the life of a civilization, it is through art that it
becomes possible for a person to acquire the mind which
prevailed elsewhere and at other times in thoroughgoing
and actual fashion.

As empirical fact, however, the arts, those of converse and the
literary arts which are the enhanced continuations of social
converse, have been the means by which goods are brought
home to human perception.[49]

Thus it appears to belong to the function of art that it
is possible for a personality to be transformed, in character
through participation in the experience of others whose
manner of living is different from his own native procedures. And so the biographical data of conversion,
regeneration, character reconstruction, and personality
transformation recorded in the testimonies of religious
devotees would seem to be practically intelligible as
natural possibilities.

The significance of art in the experience of the individual is even more comprehensively sensed when the
social bearing of its function is considered. The personal
character of each human being is directly derived from the
culture in which he participates, but this process requires
the operation of communication between persons. And it
is in the activity of communication that art contributes so
much by way of providing the means to make it feasible.

In the end, works of art are the only media of complete and
unhindered communication between man and man that can

occur in a world full of gulfs and walls that limit community of experience.[50]

Ideas are conveyed through the "external object, the product of art," which is "the connecting link between artist and audience"; but even more significantly experience is shared in communion.

For it is by activities that are shared and by language and other means of intercourse that qualities and values become common to the experience of a group of mankind. Now art is the most effective mode of communication that exists. For this reason the presence of common or general factors in conscious experience is an effect of art.[51]

Thus, the most precious values of human experience derived in social intercourse directly involve the function of art.

Every intense experience of friendship and affection completes itself artistically. The sense of communion generated by a work of art may take on a definite religious quality.[52]

Religious experience is probably the most notable manifestation of the power of art to affect profoundly the lives of men through communion.

Art is the extension of the power of rites and ceremonies to unite men, through a shared celebration, to all incidents and scenes of life. This office is the reward and seal of art. That art weds man and nature is a familiar fact. Art also renders men aware of their union with one another in origin and destiny.[53]

Dewey observes that "as the Church developed," the arts "became a bond of union among men."

But the influence that counted in the daily life of the mass of the people and gave them a sense of unity was constituted, it is safe to surmise, by sacraments, by song and pictures, by rite and ceremony, all having an esthetic strand, more than by any other one thing.[54]

Art does not intrude structures of unity or of communion into the experience of men; but by facilitating their joint activities, it enables them to share a certain mystic "esthetic surrender" in communion, and then being conscious of such communion, perceiving its form, and expressing that perception in suitable products, art exercises its office" in "remaking of the experience of the community in the direction of greater order and unity."

Art not only thus enriches the experience of men by such facilitation of communion with others, but it also functions to perpetuate values by making them available through its works at later times and in different places. In so far as education is conceived as a project whereby individuals are led into cultural participation with the civilization of any group, and into the having of the values cherished in that culture through avenues of communication, art serves this purpose to a much greater extent than is commonly recognized.

It is by way of communication that art becomes the incomparable organ of instruction, but the way is so remote from that usually associated with the idea of education.[55]

It is pertinent to note this has been eminently the case in the matter of education in religion. At the risk of being superfluous it should be noted that such "art" would not necessarily consist only of physical objects but would function in media intelligently constructed to promote the consummatory experience in mind. Thus such art products would include rites, ceremonies, sacraments, ritual, institutions, poems, music, literature, architecture, creeds, customs, etc., in fine, the whole gamut of instrumentalities conceived and construed to serve in controlling the occurrence and administering the experience of consummatory values as they have been recognized and prized.

As this discussion moves to the consideration of the meaning of religion, much that has been noted in this exposition of the meaning of art will be recalled in its bearing upon religious experience. In so far as satisfactions are had and fulfillments are felt, the esthetic experience is operative, noting and perceiving the forms involved. In so far as such perceptions are had, the effort to express them adequately to the satisfaction of the perceiver and for the benefit of others will produce artistic objects of consummatory and instrumental meaning. This is art, and it is involved in the processes of religion just as intrinsically as it has been noted in the procedures of science.

RELIGION

Perhaps the most significant trait of human experience is its ability to become conscious of its own tendencies: to become aware of phases of that stream of events which constitute the individual. Coupled with the capacity to inhibit overt and final response to problematic situations while engaging in mental processes of reflection and thought, this trait distinguishes man as a superior character of nature and enables him to achieve satisfactions and goods which sustain and enrich his experience in living far beyond what would occur apart from his creative contribution. Man is not only able to see relations between events and to construct instrumentalities to facilitate his control of the course of natural affairs, as in science; to perceive the form of consummatory experiences and to express that perception in products which enable the recurrence of such satisfactions and fulfillments, as in art; but he is able to become conscious of himself as a person, to become aware of his own identity as one unique unit of personality, to see himself in relation to his whole environment, the universe, and to dispose of his career and his destiny in comprehensive fashion by voluntary committal of himself according to belief and purpose, as in religion.

The works of Dewey do not include a comprehensive study of religious experience by analysis or exposition in experimentalist terms, but frequent and varied allusions to religion found in his major treatises serve to present a general description of this mode of human experience. The Terry lectures, published under the title *A Common Faith,* are developed upon the premise of a radical difference between the "religious" as an integral quality in any experience, and "religion" or "religions" as construed traditionally upon the basis of belief in the supernatural. In these lectures there is relatively little description or analysis of "religion" as a mode of consciousness, comparable to though distinguished from "science" and "art," in experimentalist terms that would be consonant with Dewey's thought as it is being considered in this chapter. Such a description of religion will now be undertaken at this point in this discussion.

The fundamental character of religious activity is genetically indicated to be a function of man's predicament in a hazardous, perilous world, and a significant element in the whole of human affairs:

Anthropologists have shown incontrovertibly the part played by the precarious aspect of the world in generating religion with its ceremonies, rites, cults, myths, magic; and it has shown the pervasive penetration of these affairs into morals, law, art and industry.[56]

Such a view would seem to serve as a basis for a sound analysis of the nature of religion. However, in several passages, written in historical perspective, little is added that would contribute to an adequate grasp of the meaning

of religion, while the possibility of misconception seems rather grave. Thus Dewey seems to see religion only as an irrational substitute employed in desperation by ignorant men, when he writes:

As a drowning man is said to grasp at a straw, so men who lacked the instruments and skills developed in later days, snatched at whatever, by any stretch of imagination, could be regarded as a source of help in time of trouble. The attention, interest and care which now go to acquiring skill in the use of appliances and to the invention of means for better service of ends, were devoted to noting omens, making irrelevant prognostications, performing ritualistic ceremonies and manipulating objects possessed of magical power over natural events. In such an atmosphere primitive religion was born and fostered. Rather this atmosphere *was* the religious disposition.[57]

But a close consideration of this observation will reveal that here, as elsewhere in Dewey's remarks about historic manifestations of conscious activities on the part of man, magic is properly held to be the naive alternative to science, not to religion. That it appeared in religion is a matter of record, but that it was the essence of religion does not seem to follow. As a matter of fact, in writing of this phase of human history later in the same treatise, Dewey points clearly to the meaning of religion in these words:

Being unable to cope with the world in which he lived, he sought some way to come to terms with the universe as a whole. Religion was, in its origin, an expression of this endeavor.[58]

At another point[59] in his sketch of the genetico-historical phases of religion in civilization, Dewey seems to favor the idea that the trend in human thought moved from "myths" (such as the Hebrews are held to have used) toward "reason" (such as the Greeks are conceived to have employed). By inference it would thus seem that "myths" belong to the more naive, "reason" to the more sophisticated, intellectual procedures: also it would seem to portend the disappearance of "revealed" religious tenets as men developed a more and more "rational" philosophy. Such a view would seem to hold that "faith" and "reason" are to be viewed as alternative instrumentalities; as if men with the religious problem to interpret did so first one way and then the other. It does not appear in the context that Dewey recognizes this analysis as too simple. Inasmuch as the observation seems grounded upon an interpretation of history which is not set forth in sufficient detail to permit critical appraisal, its complete consideration will not be undertaken here. The significance of religion in the activities of men, while doubtless illustrated in the cultures of the Hebrews and the Greeks, is no more to be defined by their practices than is science or art to be defined by particular developments in this or that civilization. There is doubtless a description of religious experience to be set forth in empirical experimentalist terms, and to that our thought will now be directed more specifically.

The basic situation from which Dewey's thought proceeds to the description of any phase of vital activity is that of the living organism in its environment. Though the biological aspect is characteristically taken as the normative frame of reference, this situation is held to prevail on all levels of human activity.

Morale is as much a matter of interaction of a person with his social environment as walking is an interaction of legs with a physical environment.[60]

One of the intrinsic aspects of such interactive relationship, which provides ground for understanding the origin and nature of religious experience, is the positive role of the environment in the course of living affairs. As the human

being becomes aware of this functional contribution of the environment in his own experience, an attitude is generated which seems to be basic for religion.

But I suppose that no one can deny that the sense of dependence, insisted upon, for example, by Schleiermacher, comes close to the heart of the matter.[61]

Dewey not only goes on to point out that "this sense of dependence has taken many different forms in connection with different states of culture," and to note that "history shows that there is no channel in which the sense of dependence is predestined to express itself"; but he also makes the striking observation that the modern development of scientific interpretation of the universe actually augments rather than hinders such basic attitudes.

A sense of dependence is quickened by that Copernican revolution which looks to security amid change instead of to certainty in attachment to the fixed.[62]

Such a remark is certainly in sharp contrast to the popular notion that scientific development has necessarily impaired the place of religion in the modern mind, and would seem to encourage the effort to elaborate the implications of experimental thinking in its bearing upon understanding of religious experience. It might be suggested here that if the "sense of dependence" is thus "quickened" by the ideas derived from the contribution of Copernicus, an even more profound influence seems to be potential in the contributions of Einstein, wherein "security" is to be found in direction, in orientation, in attachment, to the future.

There need be no thought here of bypassing the salutary discreditation of "magic" and "superstition" in religious ideas and practices which is properly to be held as the effect of the scientific outlook grounded in experimental thought. Doubtless much that was inadequate in religion has been exposed as worthless and properly repudiated, but here the well-worn admonition seems pertinent not to "throw the baby out with the bath water." Whatever reconstruction of religious techniques may be the consequence of the operation of intelligence as conceived in experimentalism, the basic "sense of dependence" noted above will persist and be determinative of a certain personal interest in the universe as a whole, being grounded in the very nature of the human situations.

Dewey finds corroboration for the idea of the "sense of dependence" being the basic religious attitude in the classic tradition which holds pride to be the condition which engenders evil. His humanistic outlook focuses description of the operation of pride upon the situation existing between man and man. However, the principle illustrated here is applicable in the appraisal of the malevolent influence of pride throughout the whole round of man's relationships:

The sense of dependence that is bred by recognition that the intent and effort of man are never final but are subject to the uncertainties of an indeterminate future, would render dependence universal and shared by all. It would terminate the most corroding form of spiritual pride and isolation, that which divides man from man at the foundation of life's activities. A sense of common participation in the inevitable uncertainties of existence would be coeval with a sense of common effort and shared destiny. Men will never love their enemies until they cease to have enmities. The antagonism between the actual and the ideal, the spiritual and the natural, is the source of the deepest and most injurious of all enmities.[63]

Obviously Dewey holds such "enmity" to be "actual" and to be the consequence of "pride" which is to be taken as the alternative attitude to the "sense of dependence" basic in

religious experience. That the direct inference here would point both to the validity and the significance of religion in human welfare seems unquestionable. This impression is even more thoroughly grounded in further observations which Dewey has set forth touching human consciousness of man's personal situation.

The mental capacity of man extends his environment indefinitely into the past and into the future so that he can be aware of himself as a unique event in history, living in the present moment in touch with all that affects him. Dewey has observed that the whole temporal situation is involved in the issues of every moment:

What the live creature retains from the past and what it expects from the future operate as directions in the present.[64]

The historical process extends obviously beyond the reach of the individual, while bearing down upon him in the sense of an environment that will not be denied. Yet his relationship in it is perceptible in an esthetic way.

But there is a point in *every* intelligent activity where effort ceases; where thought and doing fall back upon a course of events which effort and reflection cannot touch. There is a point *in* deliberate action where definite thought fades into the ineffable and undefinable—into emotion.[65]

Such perception of his own place in the whole course of events is intrinsically involved in the solution of the problem of living for any individual:

Only when the past ceases to trouble and anticipations of the future are not perturbing is a being wholly united with his environment and therefore fully alive.[66]

Also it serves to ground the superior worth of the consummatory experiences of the present.

Yet the last word is not with obligation nor with the future. Infinite relationships of man with his fellows and with nature already exist. The ideal means, as we have seen, a sense of these encompassing continuities with their infinite reach. This meaning even now attaches to present activities because they are set in a whole to which they belong and which belongs to them. Even in the midst of conflict, struggle and defeat a consciousness is possible of the enduring and comprehending whole.[67]

Thus it is possible for the ordinary events of physical and psychophysical interaction to acquire significance and value far beyond their actual occurrence.

Within the flickering inconsequential acts of separate selves dwells a sense of the whole which claims and dignifies them. In its presence we put off mortality and live in the universal.[68]

Dewey does not hesitate to denominate this development as the essence of religious experience.

The religious experience is a reality in so far as in the midst of effort to foresee and regulate future objects we are sustained and expanded in feebleness and failure by the sense of an enveloping whole. Peace in action not after it is the contribution of the ideal to conduct.[69]

Religion in this aspect belongs primarily to the individual in its fundamental occurrence.

Religion as a sense of the whole is the most individualized of all things, the most spontaneous, undefinable and varied. For individuality signifies unique connections in the whole.[70]

The perception of these connections involving the self and the universe is of esthetic character, which helps to explain "the historic alliance of religion and art," as it also explains the intensity of feeling that accompanies religious experience.

When the perception of the self in its total relationship is achieved esthetically as a work of art, we have the very essence of religious experience. Such consummatory appreciation of self-universe relationship is potential in "every

normal experience" and thus accounts for the ubiquity of "religious" consciousness.

In short, the thing actually at stake in any serious deliberation is not a difference of quantity, but what kind of person one is to become, what sort of self is in the making, what sort of world is making."[71]

It also provides the possibility of continuously recurring joy in the course of routine living: a fact that enhances the general esteem with which religious experience is regarded by those who have it.

Yet every act may carry within itself a consoling and supporting consciousness of the whole to which it belongs and which in some sense belongs to it. With responsibility for the intelligent determination of particular acts may go a joyful emancipation from the burden of responsibility for the whole which sustains them, giving them their final outcome and quality."[72]

Since "it is indeed true that all relations, all universals and laws as such are timeless," and that perception in its artistic form has been noted to be unique and unalterable in a final and permanent sense, the empirical ground for a sense of the eternal and unchangeable in religious experience as described above appears obvious and sound.

It is important to remember that the satisfying perception of the self-universe relationship is ideal rather than actual. Its achievement is a product of creative selection of possibilities conceived in imagination. The esthetic quality which distinguishes the form recognized in perception is one of felt harmony which becomes the source of supreme satisfaction.

Inner harmony is attained only when, by some means, terms are made with the environment. . . . Pleasures may come about through chance contact and stimulation; such pleasures are not to be despised in a world of pain. But happiness and delight are a different sort of thing. They come to be through a fulfillment that reaches to the depth of our being—one that is an adjustment of our whole being with the conditions of existence.[73]

Thus "happiness as distinct from pleasure is a condition of the self." It is to be recognized as "a stable condition, because it is dependent not upon what transiently happens to us but upon the standing disposition of the self"; and so one may find happiness in the midst of annoyances, be contented and cheerful in spite of a succession of disagreeable experiences. This satisfaction attendant upon the experience of harmony in religious perception is not however to be seized as perpetual even though its memory is a lingering pleasure.

Any attempt to perpetuate beyond its term the enjoyment attending the time of fulfillment and harmony constitutes withdrawal from the world. Hence it marks the lowering and loss of vitality. But, through the phases of perturbation and conflict, there abides the deep-seated memory of an underlying harmony, the sense of which haunts life like the sense of being founded upon a rock.[74]

Yet the recurrence of such enjoyment may be secured through intelligent activity since "nature gives, not always freely but in response to search, means and material by which the values we judge to have supreme quality may be embodied in existence." Thus the basic religious perception generates dynamic effect as man is inspired to achieve actualization, both through his own experience and through the experience of others, of the ideal possibilities visualized.

While the happy moment brings us objects to admire, approve and revere, the security and extent in which the beautiful, the true and the revered qualify the world, depend upon the way in which our own affections and desires for that kind of world engage activities. Things loved, admired and revered . . . are genuine elements of nature. But without the aid and support of

deliberate action based on understanding of conditions, they
are transitory and unstable, as well as narrow and confined in
the number of those who enjoy them."[75]

To refer to religious perceptions as ideal in distinction
from the actual is by no means to disparage their validity or
practicability. Later in this discussion Dewey's repudiation
of romanticism and subjectivism will be fully set forth in
the course of consideration of techniques of instrumentation. For the present it may suffice to note that he holds "the
religious attitude as a sense of the possibilities and as
devotion to the cause of these possibilities," and so finds
that a genuine religious outlook implies a sincere appreciation and respect for nature as it actually exists inasmuch as
it provides the means for the realization of the ideals
visualized and cherished in perception.

Religious faith which attaches itself to the possibilities of nature
and associated living would, with its devotion to the ideal,
manifest piety toward the actual. . . . Respect and esteem would
be given to that which is the means of realization of possibilities,
and to that in which the ideal is embodied if it ever finds
embodiment. Aspiration and endeavor are not ends in themselves; value is not in them in isolation but in them as means
to that reorganization of the existent in which approved meanings are attained. Nature and society include within themselves projection of ideal possibilities and contain the operations
by which they are actualized. Nature may not be worshipped as
divine even in the sense of the intellectual love of Spinoza. But
nature, including humanity, with all its defects and imperfections, may evoke heartfelt piety as the source of ideals, of possibilities, of aspiration in their behalf, and as the eventual
abode of all attained goods and excellencies."[76]

This lengthy excerpt will not only serve to establish nature
as properly estimable in the religious attitude, but it points
to the ground upon which the interplay of science, art, and

religion, as modes of handling the natural, can be seen in their complementary operation. Certainly it provides for a reciprocal respect for religion as a proper manipulation of the natural. Dewey is of the opinion that if there were no schematic intellectual commitments involved "there could be no conflict between science and religion," and goes on to say:

Whatever is discovered about actual existence would modify the content of human beliefs about ends, purposes and goods. But it would not and could not touch the fact that we are capable of directing our affection and loyalty to the possibilities resident in the actualities discovered.[77]

It is in this capacity of man to become aware of potentialities in his personal situation that religion is seen to operate and function.

It is the office of art and religion to evoke such appreciations and intimations; to enhance and steady them till they are wrought into the texture of our lives.[78]

This achievement of a perception of the self in relationship with the environing universe may be taken as the basic condition of religious experience. Both the fact that it so directly and completely involves the self, and the fact that it so comprehensively and finally involves all else in relation to the self, will explain the intensity of the feelings experienced. Such feelings can be had in any and every situation taken up in consciousness and held in ego-cosmic perspective.

Under some conditions the completeness of the object enjoyed gives the experience a quality so intense that it is justly termed religious. Peace and harmony suffuse the entire universe gathered up into the situation having a particular focus and pattern. These qualities mark any experience in as far as its final character dominates; in so far a mystic experience is simply

an accentuated intensification of a quality of experience repeatedly had in the rhythm of experiences."

Out of such supreme intensity in consummatory experience, religious values emerge as the most precious in the register of conscious appraisal. This is not to affirm any intrinsic excellency and certainly not to claim metaphysical superiority, but to recognize that in comprehensiveness of reference, in significance of practical import for the future direction of conduct, and in emotional appreciation, the objects of religious experience are esteemed above all else in the mind of man. Such prestige augments their functional import and contributes to the practical significance of religious beliefs in the affairs of men. It will serve to appreciate properly the role of intelligence in the generation of religious values to keep in mind that such values are the products of conscious experience, creatively achieved in the course of individual activity. They do not exist in some absolute sense, in some transcendental sphere, to be apprehended in recognition under certain conditions, but are the products of individual conscious experience wherein certain common natural experiences are transformed into objects of precious worth and profound dynamic significance.

The practical import of religious experience is a function of individual consciousness of the actual possibilities resident in the practical situation. Such consciousness is generated in reflection in which alternative possibilities are recognized. Intelligence is operative when these possibilities are appraised as "ends" in terms of their "foreseen consequences." Such "ends" are not extraneously found and arbitrarily imposed, "things lying beyond activity at which the latter is directed." They "arise and function within action" where "they are terminals of deliberation, and so

turning points *in* activity." The continuity of religious purposes and natural processes is thus maintained.

Ends are foreseen consequences which arise in the course of
activity and which are employed to give activity added meaning
and to direct its further course. They are in no sense ends *of*
action. In being ends of *deliberation* they are redirecting pivots
in action.[50]

In addition to the "intellectual search for ends" which
serve as devices "of intelligence in guiding action," reflective
consciousness produces "motives" which have direct dynamic bearing upon conduct. Dewey defines "motive" as
follows:

A motive is then that element in the total complex of a man's
activity which, if it be sufficiently stimulated, will result in an
act having specified consequences.

An element in an act viewed as a tendency to produce such
and such consequences is a motive. A motive does not exist
prior to an act and produce it. It is an act plus a judgment upon
some element of it, the judgment being made in the light of
the consequences of the act.[51]

Such reflection is "moral" in so far as "alternative possibilities" are recognized, "for wherever they enter a difference between better and worse arises." It becomes "religious" when the implications of an "enveloping and
expanding whole" are noted in final and ultimate terms. The
congeniality of "morals" and "religion" is thus readily seen.
Their distinction would appear to be a matter of range of
reference in the criteria of appraisal. Whereas "moral" could
conceivably be such, within particular and limited social
and specific relations, "religious" would properly involve
individual and universal relationships. In the course of the
discussion immediately following, Dewey's references to
morality will be noted in connections where he has not
made similar observations about religion, but where the

logical import of the insights set forth will be held to be as valid for religion as for morals. While there is proper discrimination on the basis of definition of scope of moral reference and religious reference, as noted above, there is no logical difference in the relationship of moral and religious to the natural, each being a quality added to natural events out of the conscious experience of the individual.

It may be well to keep in mind that it belongs to Dewey's philosophy to hold that the experience of man constitutes whatever data are to be taken and considered in reflection. That one phase of experience should be religious as herein defined, and that in that field values should be produced which are definitely art constructs rather than unaffectedly natural, does not therein jeopardize either the validity or the worth of such products. They are real, actual, existential, and nonetheless good for being artfully conceived and construed. There is no external eternal standard of absolute reality admitted, to which they must conform. Their right to be highly esteemed is grounded in the satisfactions they provide and in the consequences which they seem to bring with them. To accord such objects metaphysical status would be gratuitous and would invite fruitless controversy. They are empirical in origin and are to be taken as events occurring in life

The dynamic element seems to be even more fundamentally a function of nature itself, a characteristic trait of human nature being this impulse to seize upon that which is esteemed desirable or better.

Fidelity to the nature to which we belong, as parts however weak, demands that we cherish our desires and ideals till we have converted them into intelligence, revised them in terms of the ways and means which nature makes possible.[82]

Dewey considers this to be the judgment of common sense in reflection upon natural processes.

If it were articulate, it (common sense) would say that the same natural processes which generate goods and evils generate also the striving to secure the one and avoid the other, and generate judgments to regulate the strivings.[83]

Thus it appears that religious activity in impulse, guidance, and purpose is grounded intrinsically in the very nature of man and the universe. Aberrations, perversions, barren and harmful misconstructions in the course of human manipulation of the religious problem appear in history as the faulty works of man, but the indigenous character of religion as a proper mode of human activity with infinite potentialities of value would seem to be unquestionable.

To say that religious experience is altogether natural is to make reference to its empirical occurrence as an event or series of events causally interrelated with all other events occurring in time. It is not to dissipate the significance of the religious quality of certain events as these are had in individual consciousness. It would appear that any experience occurring in natural process can be taken in individual consciousness in its bearing upon the ultimate disposition of the self, and held in its meaning for the consummatory experiences it generates when so perceived. Thus it is invested with religious significance and becomes the ground for religious experience, which in turn generates values and purposes properly denominated religious. And so man as a natural being would find within nature the necessary ground for conceiving an essential continuity between morality and nature, and likewise religion and nature.

Dewey accepted the task of exposing this basic relationship as the proper aim of his own philosophical labors. In doing this he was addressing himself to what he considered

to be one of the greatest, if not the greatest, needs in contemporary living.

The problem of restoring integration and cooperation between
man's beliefs about the world in which he lives and his beliefs
about the values and purposes that should direct his conduct
is the deepest problem of modern life.[84]

It is not difficult to feel that such an observation points
directly to the critical importance of an understanding of
the meaning of religion from the humane practical point of
view espoused by Dewey and his experimentalist collobora-
tors. Also, the successful solution of this problem appears
sure upon the premise that man is altogether natural. By
admitting variety in nature, man can be so taken, even if
in actuality he is distinctive and superior. The problem
of integration, however, remains none the less real, being
generated by the unique, spontaneous, original traits of
human individuality; but it is soluble by the operation of
intelligence:

The effective condition of the integration of all divided purposes
and conflicts of belief is the realization that intelligent action
is the sole ultimate resource of mankind in every field whatsoever.[85]

Since every phase of human activity is basically grounded
in the various relationships and interests of the single individual, it becomes the office of reflection to effect a cor-
responding integral unity in the various activities as these
are pursued. There appears to be the possibility of failure
here, attested in such depressing fashion by the history of
human affairs; but there is likewise the possibility of success, depending upon the deliberate exercise of discriminating thinking.

Dewey presses the significance of this relationship between morality and nature, not only to the point just noted

that the operation of intelligence produces moral judgments
in the course of sound natural processes, but even further to
note that since "deliberate action, conduct into which reflective choice enters, is distinctively moral," morality is
potentially involved throughout the whole range of conscious activity. This observation supports the idea of religion being intrinsically grounded, not extra- but intra-
naturally, in all the affairs of life.

The recognition that conduct covers every act that is judged
with reference to better and worse and that the need of this
judgment is potentially coextensive with all portions of conduct,
saves us from the mistake which makes morality a separate
department of life.[86]

The domestication of moral and religious processes within
nature, by noting their basic continuity with all nature and
their possible occurrence in every phase of individual consciousness, is carried even further by Dewey when he holds
their realization to be inherently involved in the very exercise of intelligence. The very nature of man appears to
point his exercise of intelligence directly to moral and
religious judgments. This conclusion appears clearly indicated throughout Dewey's thought as the following
excerpts will show. In so far as man is competent to act
deliberately, Dewey would hold "that when man is going
to act he needs to know *what* he is going to do." This requirement can only be satisfied by an awareness of "the
quality of his act," which must be "in terms of the consequences" that will follow. But while their actualization is
thus apparently indefinite, it is by no means a matter of
indifference to man. It has been noted above that "the
actualization of meanings furnishes psychophysical qualities
with their ulterior significance and worth," and the grave
significance of that fact can scarcely be overestimated in
terms of human welfare.

As long as our own fundamental psycho-physical attitudes in dealing with external things are subconscious, our conscious attention going only to the relations of external things, so long will our perception of the external situations be subject at its root to perversion and vitiation.[87]

Dewey does not hesitate to fix responsibility upon man to qualify the course of his life.

The good, satisfaction, "end," of growth of present action in shades and scope of meaning is the only good within our control, and the only one, accordingly, for which responsibility exists.[88]

This "growth in meaning" must be an actual "present reconstructing" resulting in an additive modification of existential affairs.

Ideas are worthless except as they pass into actions which rearrange and reconstruct in some way, be it little or large, the world in which we live.[89]

Such insistence upon a practical grounding of satisfaction in achieving added meanings by actual manipulation of existential affairs is based upon the possibility of deliberate control of the occurrence of consummatory experience.

It is not a dream that it is possible to exercise some degree of regulation of the occurrence of enjoyments which are of value.[90]

As a matter of definition Dewey insists upon holding the terms "ideal" and "spiritual" to have essentially practical signification.

For the latter terms if they have any concrete application at all signify that which is a desirable consummation of conditions, a cherished fulfillment of means.[91]

It has been noted above that as the ideal relations of the self with the universe as a whole are esthetically experienced in perception, intense feelings of enjoyment having

religious quality are had. But Dewey sharply insists that
to effect such enjoyment by entertaining impractical ideals
"impossible of realization and of conception" is a "vicious"
error. This may be done in our own consciousness where

the sense of unachieved possibilities is employed as a com-
pensatory equivalent for endeavor in achievement.[92]

It may be done in the experience of others:

To "make others happy" except through liberating their powers
and engaging them in activities that enlarge the meaning of life
is to harm them and to indulge ourselves under cover of
exercising a special virtue.[93]

The inference is obvious. To be legitimately intelligent,
moral, and religious, ideas must be geared directly into the
practical administration of personal conduct: a requirement
that is held to be lodged in the very nature of man. The
volitional aspect of morals and religion is attested by "the
part played by character, by personal disposition, and attitude, in determining the direction which the intellectual
factor takes."

"Will," in the sense of unity of impulse, desire and thought
which anticipates and plans, is central in morals just because by
its very nature it is the most constant and effectual factor in
control of consequences.[94]

Such practical bearing of legitimate moral and religious
ideas provides the immediate focus of import for present
conduct, but it by no means confines the range of reference
to the local situation.

To live in the present is compatible with condensation of far-
reaching meanings in the present.[95]

This is not only true of the "experiences of the past, personal and social," as a matter of the influence of history;
but it is likewise valid in that which is specifically "reli-

gious." Dewey has remarked that "a *new religion* or a new departure in religion has often exercised a powerful influence on moral development." There need be no obscuring of the accent upon the present throughout these excerpts. It is this "immediate" emphasis, together with its "individual" orientation, that comprises the "urgency" and the "validity" of religious experience as a proper subject of philosophic consideration. Anyone interested in serving his fellow man now by identifying the processes inherent in man's present experience to the end that goods and values may be produced, improved, and shared to the mutual benefit of as many persons as it is possible to reach at this time cannot possibly doubt the pressing need of such intellectual pursuits and labors.

Perhaps the most fundamental practical import of religious processes is realized within the experience of the individual. Certainly it is in his consciousness that religious perception is esthetically enjoyed, generating the values which he comes to esteem, cherish, and seek. It is in his thought that artistic formulations of religious expression are conceived. By his intelligence religious objects are produced, which are to serve in his securing and sharing his cherished values with others. But it would seem to be even more significantly true that in so far as religious experience is legitimate and valid, its function operates primarily and initially within the structure of the individual. Since religion is being defined as the mode of conscious activity in which the self is perceived in relation to the enveloping whole of an expanding universe, it seems logically obvious that the practical bearing of such activity must focus directly upon the self. It has been remarked that the environing universe looms in obdurate fashion as embodying that which reaches beyond man's control. This is the fact that induces humility and engenders a sense of dependence. Thus it seems apparent that the immediate bearing of religious ideas will rest upon that phase of the individual situation which is susceptible to control, which is the disposition of the self in committal to chosen alternatives as visualized in the religious perceptions achieved. The generic demands of religious perception may be noted to require these alternatives to be ultimate in character, such as cosmic orientation involving eventual destiny. But it will be sufficient to note that religious thinking is so exclusively individual in its origin that it does not characteristically develop in the proximations of "measured quantities." Dewey remarks:

The nearer we come to an action that is to have an individualized unique object of experience for its conclusion, the less do we think the things in question in these exclusively metric terms (having reference to science).[96]

And yet, however unique may be the initial aspect and fundamental character of religious experience within the individual consciousness, it cannot remain exclusively ineffable in any mystic sense either as a subject of thought or as a significant mode of activity. The consummatory quality will indeed be indescribable, but the description of genetic conditions, expressive formulations, and anticipated consequences, which is the intellectualization of the content of religious experience, is necessarily a social matter.

It may be helpful at this point to interpolate an observation regarding certain characteristics manifest in Dewey's thought which tend to complicate the elaboration of the communal aspects of religious experience. The definitive description of religion as a mode of conscious activity has thus far been set forth largely in the biological terminology so generally employed by Dewey. It is quite probable that an unconscious tendency to limit meanings being conveyed to the specific perspective of biology may seem to suggest

inadequacy in the description offered. The adequate pre-
caution to avoid such misconception is a constant reminder
of the precise sense in which Dewey uses such terms as
"nature," "environment," "objects," "goods," etc. It belongs
to Dewey's naturalistic empirical approach that language
be impersonal, but there is no necessity that personality
be deemed suspect. Dewey intends no schematic restriction
to the physiological nor even to the psychophysical. Doubtless the thought of Dewey seems cumbersome in referring
to human personality. His characteristic aversion to referring directly to anything metaphysical will account for
the absence of reference to individual identities. It is never
quite clear to what extent any individual is an entity. The
biological organism is seen to exist in singular fashion as
a complex of events, comprised of a multitude of elemental
factors, yet constituted a unit under the aegis of the vital
condition of life. It is seen as distinctly temporal. But the
problem of the person is more obscure and difficult of
comprehension. Without pausing here to engage in elaboration of detail, it would seem proper to say that in Dewey's
description at best the "self" is an object conceived and
construed in the conscious processes wherein nature experiences itself. That this "self" is then conceived as mutually and intimately related to the specific physical organism
in a unique and particular sense seems to be the function of
"self-consciousness." Thus at the most a "person" would
seem to be an esthetic perception of a unique pattern of
events centered in the single biological organism. And so all
"persons" are to be taken as "self-made" as one peculiar
manifestation of natural process. The rigorous empiricism of
Dewey prohibits any intimation that such a "person" is
any more than an arrangement of constituent elements. Yet
in his analysis of art, Dewey has recognized the origin and
persistence of permanent forms which are additive accre-

tions to the sum total of the universe. Logically such status would seem available for "personal forms." But Dewey does not seem to have granted definite recognition to such entities in his works. It would seem that Dewey's intellectual outlook affords only the suggestion of "animism" to account for the human practice of ascribing "personality" to natural objects such as himself and others he esteems to be like himself. In fact it may be a proper question in the light of Dewey's distinctive approach whether personality should be ascribed to events occuring outside of the self. Yet when the term is held to be indicative of a certain character of event defined as "persons," its adjectival nature is apparently sufficiently obvious to warrant such usage. There is no intimation in this denotation of identifying units of personality beyond indicative reference to continuous histories. That such technical designation would prove inadequate and unsuitable for the converse of affection and esteem may well be the case. But it is a mode of classification congenial to the philosophy of Dewey, where it apparently serves the purpose for which that philosophy has been conceived.

To whatever actually exists which is denominated "person," Dewey accords full empirical status. The distinctive character of human experience, and the empirical actuality of the social process, are freely and respectfully recognized. Thus "nature" and "environment" are held to include whatever "persons" and "personalities" are. In the consciousness of man social relations are held as existential and as such they are taken in their bearing upon the fortunes and welfare of the individual. William James advanced the idea that man's interest in social approach of himself led to theistic conception of the universe.⁷ However, until some adequate insight into the problem of human personality is established, as founded in Dewey's philosophical expressions, it would be idle to propose an appraisal of any

conception of God as a "person" in experimentalist terms.
This does not imply that Dewey holds any adverse position any more than it is implied that the wife of one's
bosom is to be held as only an animistic ascription of "personality" to a "complex of energies" with which one is tem-
porarily related in biological and practical propinquity.
Dewey has invariably respected and dignified man as the
highest form in nature, possessing unique and distinguishing traits of the highest order. He has always appreciated
the superior significance of social values. There would seem
to be no ground to anticipate that he is committed to such
intellectual positions as would lead him to disparage that
in the universe which could be recognized as "higher than
I."

Despite the obscurity in his works regarding the nature
of personality which has just been noted, Dewey has clearly
recognized the operation of social processes in human
experience. Mental processes are seen to be grounded in
social interaction as individuals artfully achieve communication and communion by the use of instrumentalities
such as language, symbols, etc. While nothing can be so
precious as the ineffable, spontaneous, consummatory individual experience, there would be no security of control,
no assurance of understanding, no improvement by intelligence, nor even enrichment through appreciation, without
the achievement of instrumental media which will facilitate
social interactive processes out of which beliefs, values,
and purposes arise as cultural objects.

This is as true in religion as in other modes of conscious
activity. It will be the further aim in this discussion to
consider what is involved in the instrumentation aspect of
religious experience, but it is pertinent in this phase of interpretation to note that much of the notoriety so commonly ascribed to religion as being conservative, reaction-

ary, outmoded, is actually cultural rather than religious, and is a function of society rather than of the individual. Thus Dewey observes:

Consciousness of the whole has been connected with reverences, affections and loyalties which are communal. But special ways of expressing the communal sense have been established. . . . Religion has lost itself in cults, dogmas and myths.[64]

Apparently this denaturing development occurred in the course of stereotyping under the social tendency toward conformity in which individual spontaneity is largely submerged. Dewey goes on to remark that while "religion as a sense of the whole is the most individualized of all things, the most spontaneous, undefinable, and varied" (and it may be kept in mind that such in its primal character it will ever be as it emerges in consciousness),

Yet it has been perverted into something uniform and immutable. It has been formulated into fixed and defined beliefs expressed in required acts and ceremonies. Instead of marking the freedom and peace of the individual as a member of an infinite whole, it has been petrified into a slavery of thought and sentiment, an intolerant superiority on the part of a few and an intolerable burden on the part of many.[66]

Surely it will not require elaborate argument to maintain that this cultural plight, which has beset the public formulations of religious expression in belief and practice, has no more genetic connection with religion than the Ptolemaic cosmogony had with science. What Copernicus and Galileo did for science in founding an outlook and a method which eventually freed science from the impediments of philosophical accretions which were obstructing its development and hindering its efficacy may need to be done for religion. But it is not religion that is at fault in this matter. Dewey voices an optimistic confidence in the eventual achievement of such needed liberations:

The religious attitude as a sense of the possibilities and as devotion to the cause of these possibilities, as distinct from acceptance of what is given at the time, gradually extricates itself from these unnecessary intellectual commitments.[100]

But he recognizes that "religious devotees rarely stop to notice that what lies at the basis of recurrent conflicts with scientific findings is not this or that special dogma so much as it is alliance with philosophical schemes." This observation supports the view that such which has been laid to the intellectual discredit of religion belongs essentially to cultural processes rather than to religion in its characteristic mode.

The tendency to resist change, while appearing in religion, does not seem to be peculiar to that mode of activity but is to be better understood as a philosophical trait:

Beliefs current in morals, politics, and religion, are marked by dread of change and by the feeling that order and regulative authority can be had only through reference to fixed standards accepted as finalities, because referring to fixed antecedent realities.[101]

It is quite possible that so far from being inherently natural, this trait emerges as one of the unintended consequences of art. The communicating powers of art are so extensive that they operate to establish a community between individuals now living in whose spontaneity vital changes are potential, and others already dead whose structures must perforce remain constant:

Rite and ceremony as well as legend bound the living and the dead in a common partnership.[102]

The grounding of such community does not seem to be hindered by the unilateral aspect in which the living supply all the initiative and make all the adjustments.

Friendship and intimate affection are not the result of information about another person even though knowledge may further their formation. . . . It is when the desires and aims, the interests and modes of response of another become an expansion of our own being that we understand him. We learn to see with his eyes, hear with his ears, and their results give us true instruction, for they are built into our own structure.[103]

In so far as the forms of such communal experience are standardized and fixed by cultural products into instrumentalities devised to suit the needs of historical situations no longer extant, there is something distinctly suitable in their description as "dead." It is at this point that the reconstructing operation of continuing intelligence is so critically demanded:

What is needed is intelligent examination of the consequences that are actually effected by inherited institutions and customs, in order that there may be intelligent consideration of the ways in which they are to be intentionally modified in behalf of generation of different consequences.[104]

Whether such modification needs to be anticipated for every cultural structure would probably require a closer examination of what is involved with reference to art products of the "classic" variety. But that all the heritage of the past should be so subjected to experimental testing in the interests of maximum present benefits would seem a warrantable conclusion.

Nevertheless Dewey recognizes a popular aversion to such procedure even though he does not admit the objection rests upon valid grounds.

But, generally speaking, the idea of actively adopting experimental method in social affairs, in the matters deemed of most enduring and ultimate worth, strikes most persons as a surrender of all standards and regulative authority. But in principle, experimental method does not signify random and aimless action; it implies direction by ideas and knowledge. The question at

issue is a practical one. Are there in existence the ideas and the knowledge that permit experimental method to be effectively used in social interests and affairs? [105]

It would appear in answer to this query that since the idea of experimental intelligence set forth by Professor Dewey himself is intrinsically grounded in the nature of man, therefore it is to be held as inherently applicable for the direction of religious experience to the advantage of all men. This view rests upon the impressive record of experimental science as a mode of controlling natural processes to the achievement of preferred goods. The incidental development of science in the realm of the physical does not confine its validity as method to that plane of events. Dewey has remarked:

> But a moral that frames its judgments of value on the basis of consequences must depend in a most intimate manner upon the conclusions of science. For the knowledge of the relations between changes which enable us to connect things as antecedents and consequences *is* science. [106]

Such an observation would seem to remove the last possible vestige of philosophical doubt as to the possibility of extending the application of scientific method to the investigation and manipulation of religious experience.

The popular aversion to the use of experimental methods in dealing with social affairs is probably generated in the inability of common sense adequately to grasp the significance of sophisticated methods and results. Dewey has discussed this inability in the case of the physical sciences[107] where he warns against the uncritical acceptance of the material of naïve observation unaided by exact instruments. He points out that modern science has immeasurably increased its efficiency by development of technical instrumentalities which aid, verify, and correct the natural senses, even though in so doing technical conclusions are reached which seem strange, incredible, and often quite unintelligible to the unsophisticated mind. There would seem to be no logical restriction to prevent the application of this insight in the matter of an intellectualization of religion. Here, as elsewhere, more exact, more highly developed technical grasp of the procedures of religion in terms of refined concepts would be the mark of more efficient, more intelligent comprehension. The offhand snap judgments of minds unacquainted with empirical religious phenomena and untrained in the suitable techniques of analysis and interpretation can be accorded no more rating in this field of human experience than in any other. It need scarcely be stressed that competence and skill in the understanding and manipulation of religious experience is specifically acquired and does not exist as a function of general intelligence nor as an indirect ability derived from intellectual attainments in some other field.

This sketch of the meaning of religion has been set forth in the judgment that the problem of the reality of religious experience is more urgent than the matter of definition. The traditional analysis of conscious activity into science, art, and religion seems clearly to be continued in Dewey's philosophical expositions, wherein he has dwelt more seriously upon science and art. The threefold discrimination in human interest is observed to generate science as a mode of activity to achieve delight in satisfactions, and religion as a mode of activity to achieve security of being, of existence in a precarious world. Thus religion appears grounded in man's preoccupation with himself, his fortunes, his welfare, his character, his destiny. That all three modes develop specific intellectual perspectives and techniques along their respective particular lines will account for divergence and dissimilarity in results, emphases, values, etc. But the situation in which the one individual con-

sciousness generates the several modes of interest and activity, the one biological organism provides the natural ground for each intellectual structure in its own organic environmental interactions, and the one personal identity is involved in the consequences of each and every various action undertaken points to a "practical and human" need for integration of all "specialized results." "The need for direction of action in large social fields" has been held by Dewey as "the source of a genuine demand for unification of scientific conclusions," which may be expected to follow "when their bearing on the conduct of life is disclosed." A recognition of the meaning of religion as set forth in this exposition of Dewey's interpretation of human experience will point directly to the reinstatement of religion as an important and significant mode of conscious interest and activity.

That religion as a natural human mode of action is suitable for the operation of intelligence as set forth in the philosophical thought of John Dewey would seem to follow without question. Thus the achievement, improvement, and distribution of its values may be expected to follow directly upon efficient instrumentation as a result of the exercise of intelligent thought. It is to this practical phase of philosophical interest that this discussion will now turn, in the confidence that intellectual analysis will discover that appropriate procedures will generate and promote religious experience.

VI: INSTRUMENTATION IN RELIGIOUS EXPERIENCE

Dewey has noted the initial phase of intellectual activity to be one of interpretation in which structures, processes, and principles are recognized, described, and known for what they signify in the total situation which is being taken in hand. Interpretation may be considered as having achieved its purpose when ends have been identified as ends-in-view and the whole problematic situation so understood that there is appreciation of the values and goods preferred and understanding of actual conditions and potential procedures which can serve as means to procure the consequences desired. Interpretation is consciously and openly preliminary to the eventual having such consummatory experiences as are prized and cherished by man. The exposition thus far has been pointed to an interpretation of religious experience as a natural human affair, empirically real, and vitally significant in the fortunes, welfare, and happiness of mankind. The aim has been to show the grounds on which religious experience can be intellectualized just as any other mode of conscious activity, and its occurrence realized, amplified, and guided by intelligent instrumentation. It is to this second practical phase of intellection the discussion will now turn to show that experimental procedures are valid and effectual here also, in direct proportion to the intelligence exercised.

Instrumentation is an eminently practical phase of intelligent effort to achieve and secure by theoretical and technical procedures such goods as are empirically constituted

in the consummatory enjoyments and satisfactions of man. The issue of the intrinsic or ultimate validity or authenticity of such goods is not at stake here. Dewey has indicated the distinctively practical character which properly belongs to theoretical criticism:

Meantime the work which theoretical criticism might do has not been done; namely, discovery of the conditions and consequences, the existential relations, of goods which are accepted as goods, not because of theory but because they are such in experience.[1]

Thus it seems clear that in so far as religious values are had and esteemed by man, the problem of their realization looms as a proper task for such intelligence as man may achieve through experimental thinking in the situation where such values arise. It doubtless belongs to the pragmatic character of Dewey's intellectual interests that he should appreciate this crucial role of intelligence to such an extent as to accord it the highest importance, thus making it the supreme value in his estimation.

Because intelligence is critical method applied to goods of belief, appreciation and conduct, so as to construct freer and more secure goods, turning assent and assertion into free communication of shareable meanings, turning feeling into ordered and liberal sense, turning reaction into response, it is the reasonable object of our deepest faith and loyalty, the stay and support of all reasonable hopes.[2]

While the logic in such a judgment which raises an instrumental character to a place of highest esteem may challenge closer scrutiny, there need be no mistaking the appreciation of the role of intelligence as method in the securing of goods. Perhaps something of the ground for Dewey's high esteem of intelligence in human affairs is hinted in this comment, wherein the need of some general principle for clarifying the confusion resulting from sophisticated specialization is recognized:

Over-specialization and division of interests, occupations and goods create the need for a generalized medium of intercommunication, of mutual criticism through all-around translation from one separated region of experience into another.[3]

When it is recalled that elsewhere Dewey has remarked that "practical and human need" constitutes "a genuine demand for unification of scientific conclusions" and then goes on to say "they are organized when their bearing on the conduct of life is disclosed," the intimate connection between intelligence and morals, or even religion, in the perspective of experimental thinking seems strongly indicated. Such would seem to be the burden of his personal manifesto in *A Common Faith.* It certainly is a judgment to which he has given reiterated expression throughout his more formal philosophical works. Dewey seems to feel that the importance of this relationship underlies the greatest issue in contemporary culture, as indicated in this passage noted above:

The problem of restoring integration and cooperation between man's beliefs about the world in which he lives and his beliefs about the values and purposes that should direct his conduct is the deepest problem of modern life.[4]

That such recognition of the supreme role of intelligence in the practical affairs of men may result in mistaking intellectual objects as the only realities is pointed out in the following lengthy excerpt in which Dewey at the same time indicates the enriching, additive significance of intelligent operations:

Reflective knowledge is the *only* means of regulation. Its value as instrumental is unique. Consequently philosophers, themselves occupied in a fascinating branch of reflective knowledge, have isolated knowledge and its results. They have

ignored its context of origin and function and made it coextensive with all valid experience. The doctrine was thus formed that all experience of worth is inherently cognitive; that other modes of experienced objects are to be tested, not here and there as occasion demands but universally by reduction to the terms of known objects. This assumption of the proper ubiquity of knowledge is the great intellectualistic fallacy. It is the source of all disparagement of everyday qualitative experience, practical, esthetic, moral. It is the ultimate source of the doctrine that calls subjective and phenomenal all objects of experience that cannot be reduced to properties of objects of knowledge.

From this derogation of the things we experience by way of love, desire, hope, fear, purpose and the traits characteristic of human individuality, we are saved by the realization of the purposefully instrumental and abstract character of objects of reflective knowledge. One mode of experience is as real as any other. But apart from the exercise of intelligence which yields knowledge, the realities of our emotional and practical life have fragmentary and inconsistent meanings and are at the mercy of forces beyond our control. We have no choice save to accept them or flee from them. Experience of that phase of objects which is constituted by their relations, their interactions, with one another, makes possible a new way of dealing with them, and thus eventually creates a new kind of experienced objects, not more real than those which preceded but more significant, and less overwhelming and oppressive.[5]

This observation is illustrated in the field of religious experience where, for example, reflective attention first discovers relations in worship activities and then objectifies them as patterns of procedures to be deliberately undertaken toward the securing of more worship experiences. Such "programs of worship," "orders of service," are not so impressive in themselves as the experiences they induce. They are just as real, and in a practical sense more significant, because they are available for the repeated having of further worship experiences at will. Dewey's observation points further to the fact that worship experiences which are had as a result of such intelligent instrumentalities are actually of better quality. His thought is expressed in a comment wherein he holds "science, morals and esthetic appreciation" to be similarly susceptible to the additive effect of operative intelligence.

All alike exhibit the difference between immediate goods casually occurring and immediate goods which have been reflectively determined by means of critical inquiry. . . . All cases manifest the same duality and present the same problem; that of embodying intelligence in action which shall convert casual natural goods, whose causes and effects are unknown, into goods valid for thought, right for conduct and cultivated for appreciation.[6]

The artistic origin of instrumentalities construed in intelligent method as mechanisms of procedure has such far-reaching significance for an understanding of religious practices that further exposition of their character seems warranted. While intelligence is doubtless the formative principle directing the processes of instrumentation, determining the structures produced, and developing the procedures employed, the original element is always gross experience had by man in the natural course of events. Effective instrumentalities are properly held to be more than natural, but are to be thought of as distinctive additions rather than as arbitrary intrusions of some genetically disparate character. Dewey points out their empirical source in the cognition of existential relations connecting actual events:

To the original gross experience of things there is superadded another type of experience, the product of deliberate art, of which *relations* rather than qualities are the significant subject-matter. These connections are as much experienced as are the

qualitatively diverse and irreducible objects of original natural experience.[7]

Thus it follows that such objects are admittedly different in character from naive experience even though they are based on the common natural affairs which constitute the whole life of man. Their distinction is to be seen in the nature of their significance which derives not from intrinsic quality but rather from instrumental import.

At this point an interesting observation by Dewey suggests a much more generous attitude in appraisal of instrumentalities employed in the promotion of religious experience than is generally maintained in critical analysis of religious techniques and procedures. Dewey writes:

A poor tool is often better than none at all. It has even been doubted whether any hypothesis ever entertained has not turned out later to have been erroneous in important aspects. It is still questioned whether many of the objects of the most valuable and indispensable hypothesis in present use have actual existence; the existential status of the electron is still, for example, a matter of controversy.[8]

Without pressing this comment to endorse anything fantastic or patently false, and without basing here any latitudinarian indifference as to integrity and authenticity of means, the implication seems properly drawn that a stubborn skepticism which demands that every item in an idea must be verified beyond any shadow of doubt is simply a case of shortsighted failure to appreciate the instrumental character of the means in question. Pragmatic evidence of efficacy would seem to be sufficient to establish instrumental validity. Much of the currently popular adverse criticism of the instrumentalities employed by the propagators of religious experience in so far as it is grounded upon analytic investigation of the intrinsic merits of methods and techniques is by so much beside the point, and may thus properly be ignored in the elaboration of an experimental understanding of the instrumentation of religious aims and purposes. The principle involved has profound practical bearing upon the whole discussion in hand, yet it can be stated in simple terms. Not original conditions, not primal constituents, not historical connotations, but eventual consequences comprise the proper data for evaluation of religious customs and practices. It has been noted above that Dewey makes this plain:

The fact is that an idea, intellectually, cannot be defined by its structure, but only by its function and use.*

This observation grounds an unprejudiced intellectual approach to the study of religious techniques and provides a basis for considerable economic advantage in the conservation of interest and energy in the direction and guidance of reflection and consideration.

As a matter of fact, inasmuch as the goods, which as consequences give instrumental significance to things held as antecedents, have empirical origin in the spontaneous, unique consummatory enjoyments and satisfactions of individuals, there would seem to be no purely theoretical criteria by which any instrumentality can be appraised. Apparently such value is constituted in the experience of man and by his own estimation of the preciousness of the satisfactions which he derives therefrom. Neither does there seem to be any proper metaphysical issue. Since values are established in the esteem of man, it would appear that no external absolute criterion exists by which the instrumentalities employed to secure values can be appraised as such. Their significance is obviously one of practical import, which can be exposed. Their ultimate valuation is dependent upon the spontaneous judgments of individual esteem which must in the nature of things remain inscrutable.

And so the line of inquiry leads directly to the consideration of the instrumentalities themselves, accepting them in their operative significance without discount based on any depreciation of the goods they are construed to secure. The goods of religion may be lightly esteemed on any ground whatsoever, but the intrumental efficacy of means employed remains a proper subject of intellectual interest in any project of experimental research.

It is to be noted that activities and practices which acquire instrumental significance are such as occur naturally in the interactions of organic behavior:

A genuine instrumentality *for* is always an organ *of* an end.[16]

The acquisition of meaning is the product of intelligent reflection upon actual experience. The course of such reflection follows expanding connections into ever larger relationships in which the particular thing acquires wider and other significance.

Since all knowing, including all scientific inquiry, aims at clothing things and events with meaning—at understanding them—it always proceeds by taking the thing inquired into out of its isolation. Search is continued until the thing is discovered to be a related part in some larger whole.[11]

It is important to note, however, that such significance must have been potential in the very nature of things. It is impossible by arbitrary intellectual procedure to invest extraneous material with competent meaning.

Intense and vivid realization of the meanings of the events and situations of the universe can be achieved only through a medium already instinct with meaning.[12]

There is implied here a natural limitation upon the processes of instrumentation, serving to hold all intellectualization closely to the original experience of man, which reflection may properly undertake to improve but not to deny or to displace.

If religious experience is had by man, producing goods and values which he cherishes, intelligent research may discover causal conditions, reflection may conceive ideas of instrumental relationships and construe structures to serve as mechanisms of manipulation and control; but to be experimentally valid all such intellection must deal with actual occurrences. Instrumentation is a phase of art, and in religious matters manifests the character of art as it does in any other field. Thus it is characteristic that religious instrumentalities should utilize media peculiarly suited to the purpose in view. Such media may be chosen and developed under the aegis of intelligence, but they will appear as artful constructs of that which belongs intrinsically to the production of the goods desired.

The use of a particular medium, a special language having its own characteristics, is the source of every art, philosophic, scientific, technological and esthetic. The arts of science, of politics, of history, and of painting and poetry all have finally the same *material;* that which is constituted by the interaction of the live creature with his surroundings. They differ in the media by which they convey and express this material, not in the material itself. Each one transforms some phase of the raw material of experience into new objects according to the purpose, each purpose demands a particular medium for its execution.[13]

Dewey does not specifically name religion in this passage but the applicability of the observation to religious processes is unquestionable. In so far as religious experience is distinct, its artful promotion will employ unique media, which however are not foreign to the experience desired but rather peculiarly suited because intrinsically inherent in that particular mode of activity. It need

scarcely be noted in any special way that religious goods can be secured only by the exercise of religious practices. The attempt to achieve the benefits of religion by procedures developed for and suited to enterprises which may distinctively be termed secular can not be held as intelligent. And from this point of view it must also be considered equally true that it is not possible to deny authentic religious procedures the legitimate use of media specifically designed to accomplish the religious purpose in view. This idea is stated by Dewey in terms of art, but is properly taken as valid for religious instrumentation:

In every work of art, however, these meanings are actually embodied in a material which thereby becomes the medium for their expression.[14]

That religious instrumentalities should not be held as immune to criticism but as suitable to intelligent reconstruction with a view to increasing their efficiency is to be understood without question. But it belongs to the experimental philosophy of John Dewey to insist that as religious instrumentalities are produced in the course of religious experience they are to be tested, checked, modified, and reconstructed within that mode of activity. It simply does not belong to the competence of abstract intellectualization to pass upon the validity or efficacy of religious instruments. Such reflection may serve to produce hypotheses looking toward verification and improvement, but here as in all other phases of human experience it remains as Dewey has observed:

The acquisition of definiteness and of consistency of meanings is derived primarily from practical activities.[15]

There is a mode of logical experimentation which is properly taken as "practical activity," but the conclusion seems warranted that any considerable or serious alteration of religious practices must originate and develop in the experience of those who deliberately employ them. It is the claim of this discussion that philosophical understanding of religious processes in experimental terms will facilitate and promote such improvement and development of religious experience as is designated by the term education. The very fact that instrumentalities are so directly produced by the exercise of spontaneous individual intelligence accounts both for the peril of potential aberration, perversion, etc., making experimental verification a constant requirement, and for the possibility of creative improvement, refinement, etc. But above all it emphasizes the importance of effectual educational procedure.

Activities commonly recognized as religious practices can well be taken as procedures employing instrumentalities for the generation and promotion of religious experience. An analytic survey of their empirical occurrence will identify at least three general characters of procedure as (1) acts of worship, which are primarily an individual matter, (2) order of ritual, which is largely a social communal affair, and (3) plan of creed, which is formally intellectual but designed for practical purposes. That worship, ritual, and creed are manifestly involved in religion is a matter of common reference. That they are empirically practiced as procedures having both immediate and relational qualities, and that their instrumental aspect is the more significant, is the position taken in this exposition. It will be the aim of this further discussion to show that the validity of their instrumental character and the nature of their operative relations manifest the exercise of experimental intelligence.

Religious experience has been defined as that mode of consciousness in which the relationship of the self to the universe as a whole constitutes the determinant ele-

ment. Dewey's conceptions of nature as existing in infinite relationships both actual and potential, and of man as a unique mode of nature capable of experiencing himself in his manifold relationships, ground the validity of religious experience. As man becomes aware of himself as an integral part of the universe and of his possibilities in terms of future experience and eventual destiny, he is enabled to arrive at a perception of himself related in some satisfying way to that which is greater than he. Such perception entails esthetic enjoyment and appreciation. Inasmuch as the perception involves himself in the most complete and drastic fashion, the feelings and emotions aroused are of the keenest and deepest sort. Likewise the joy involved becomes a supreme value to be cherished and sought after. This experience of such perception may be termed "worship," being essentially an esthetic appreciation of the perception which involves the self in relationships, which in turn produce the highest values cherished by man.

It is apparent that such definition of "worship" permits the term to be used in designating widely variant experiences, limited only by the actual judgment of men as they produce first this value and then that in a certain free spontaneity. And to this the empirical facts in human history obviously concur. Men may formulate their values in sensual indulgence, in grotesque imagining, in superstitious fear, in sentimentality, in rationality, in cupidity, in tradition—in fine, in any mode of interest. There seems to be no intrinsic principle that would determine the level at which values must appear. And so it follows that men may "worship" anything, which as a matter of record they are known to do. However, by this definition it is held that values cherished in worship are esteemed to be the highest, the greatest, in that they comprise the most satisfying experience man believes he can have. The fact that such evaluation of the ensuing experience may be perverse, inadequate, faulty, is a matter to be determined in intelligent reflection and critical examination, but that such perceptions of value do exist generates their appreciation as "worship."

It has been noted above that esthetic enjoyment is markedly exuberant in moments of achievement. Consciousness invariably implies some sort of reconstruction under way. Awareness seems to be the sensing of alternatives, the recognition of problematic situations. Thinking is an experimental investigation of the potential alternatives leading to settled conclusions. Thus religious consciousness would be an awareness of something dubious about the status or security of the self, and "worship" would be the moment of exuberant joy in some perception achieved by the committing of one's self to a structure of relations which produce the satisfactions desired. There is no difficulty in recognizing the precarious circumstances in which living occurs as the source of that general and deep uneasiness which "haunts the soul" and generates the awareness of uncertainty and foreboding, as the implications of present conditions are recognized in terms of dire possibilities. The very fact that such prospect is basically lodged in man's environment, before which he is largely helpless, induces that "sense of dependence" which has been noted as being the root of religious experience. The fact that some disagreeable consequences have already befallen man shatters any complacency which may have been enjoyed in wishful thinking. The obdurate character of the natural situation discourages shallow optimism. This is the origin of that fear which Dewey concedes may well have inspired religion universally among men. This is not any artificial fear aroused in superstition but an actual,

natural, grounded apprehension which may have produced superstition, attempts at magic, and all the grotesque imaginings of fearful minds, but which in itself had authentic origin in valid recognition of genuine peril. It belongs to the vital interest of the organism to seek those elements in the environment which may serve as means toward escape from peril, in the achieving of security and satisfaction. Such search is undertaken in all the urgency of the struggle and battle to live. When some element has been identified as that which will save and satisfy there is the immediate, exuberant, exhilarant sense of triumph and victory in that moment of perception in which the self is seen as actually committed to that element in a definite structure of effectual relationships.

Dewey has pointed out that "every mode of awareness . . . in its immediate existence is . . . a remaking of meanings of events." Thus the very situation which has aroused consciousness carries within it the elements out of which through reconstruction and redirection by means of knowledge a new and different situation may be produced, as was noted above in this discussion.

But we know with respect to any subject matter whatsoever in the degree in which we are able deliberately to transform doubtful situations into resolved ones.[16]

"Operational thinking needs to be applied" in the very situation which aroused consciousness. The fact that such a situation is ideal in character does not preclude the demand for "experimental empiricism" in the search for satisfying and satisfactory conclusions, because in experimental thinking it is to be remembered that concepts were regarded as designations of operations to be performed.[17]

Caution is required here to avoid the grievous error

of wishful thinking in which unreal possibilities are conceived and enjoyed apart from existential potentialities. This seems to be the character of a certain idealism which debauches the thinking of some who are aware of the human predicament, but who have entangled themselves in an "unreal mixture of thought and emotion" by neglecting the basic grounding of all significant intellection in practical affairs. Dewey describes the origin and nature of this mistaken idea in these words:

Idealistic revolt is blind and like every blind reaction sweeps us away. The quality of the idol is exalted till it is something beyond all possibility of definite plan and execution. Its sublimity renders it inaccessibly remote. An ideal becomes a synonym for whatever is inspiring—and impossible. Then, since intelligence cannot be wholly suppressed, the ideal is hardened by thought into some high, far-away object. It is so elevated and so distant that it does not belong to this world or to experience. It is in technical language, transcendental; in common speech, supernatural, of heaven not of earth. The ideal is then a goal of final, exhaustive, comprehensive perfection which can be defined only by complete contrast with the actual. Although impossible of realization and of conception, it is still regarded as the source of all generous discontent with actualities and of all inspiration to progress.

This notion of the nature and office of ideals combines in one contradictory whole all that is vicious in the separation of desire and thought.[18]

Although such futile thinking may seem to honor "virtue" by conceiving the "desirable" in terms of "perfection" so exquisite as to be unattainable, Dewey is unrelenting in his exposé of its intrinsic unsoundness.

Whatever is peculiarly romantic excites a feeling that the possibilities suggested go beyond not merely actual present realization, but are beyond effective attainment in any ex-

perience. In so far intentionally romantic art is wilful, and in so far not art. Excited and uneasy perceptual enjoyment is made ultimate, and the work of art is accommodated to production of these feelings.[19]

There is no denying that the production of phantasy and illusion involves a certain change within the self and occasions a certain kind of enjoyment. But the whole weight of experimental thinking is definitely against accepting any such impractical, visionary conceptualization as worthy or valid for man. It is of particular importance that this observation be made clear in this matter of "worship," because of the widespread notoriety which just such visionary practices have brought upon all religion. Thus Dewey writes:

This constant throwing of emphasis back upon a change made in ourselves instead of one made in the world in which we live seems to me the essence of what is objectionable in "subjectivism" . . . . All the theories which put conversion "of the eye of the soul" in the place of a conversion of natural and social objects that modifies goods actually experienced, is a retreat and escape from existence—and this retraction into self is, once more, the heart of subjective egoisms. The typical example is perhaps the other-worldliness found in religions whose chief concern is with the salvation of the personal soul. But other-worldliness is found as well in estheticism and in all seclusion within ivory towers.[20]

The import of this comment is perhaps unmistakable, and yet several observations need to be made to avoid misapplication. Dewey's basic assumption that man is within nature, within the world, together with his insistence that "thinking" changes the world, would seem to support the thesis that any change in the "self" is a change in the world. To reconcile the above excerpt as it stands with Dewey's general view as it has been now recounted, it is necessary to understand "salvation of the personal soul" to be a matter *unrelated* to life in its actual affairs. It is obvious that Dewey is not tilting his lance particularly at religion, even though he does specifically make his point clear by such reference to that field of experience. Also in his more general remark some clarification seems in order. Deprecation of "ivory towers" must obviously not be taken to refer to secret seclusion within highly technical laboratories where preoccupation with specialized theoretical abstractions has featured the sophistication of scientific method and has produced practical benefits of the widest range. Dewey must be understood to have used this term in an idiomatic sense. As pertinent as this insight is, in its salutary demand that all conceptualization be related to actual issues arising in practical affairs, it must not be taken to disparage refined and sophisticated techniques and practices developed for the purpose of achieving creative decisions within religious consciousness.

That Dewey had no intention of leaving such an erroneous impression is obvious from the following comment offered subsequently in this immediate context:

It is not in the least implied that change in personal attitudes, in the disposition of the "subject," is not of great importance. Such change, on the contrary, is involved in any attempt to modify the conditions of the environment. But there is a radical difference between a change in the self that is cultivated and valued as an end, and one that is a means to alteration, through action, of objective conditions.[21]

Here again, while the point emphasized is obvious, there is need for caution against error in understanding what is meant. Apparently Dewey intends the major accent to rest upon the instrumental significance of such change in its bearing upon the practical welfare of the subject. He would subordinate immediate enjoyment to eventual ef-

ficacy, and to such discipline must be accorded every approval. In another context Dewey has remarked:

All genuine education *terminates* in discipline, but it *proceeds* by engaging the mind in activities worth while for their own sake.[22]

With such emphasis there can be no complaint. However, though the instrumental significance be thus properly held as the more important, there need be no aspersion cast upon "change" because it affords an immediate satisfaction. The art-character of the perception involved in conceiving the "change" as desirable yields an esthetic enjoyment here just as it would in any kind of problem. Doubtless there may be ground for according this aspect only this minimal consideration in view of the unwholesome effect of all "daydreaming" and phantasy. Yet such remarks should not be permitted to render all consummatory experience suspect. Dewey has noted:

There may occur . . . process and product that are characteristically excellent. This occurs when activity is productive of an object that affords continuously renewed delight. This condition requires that the object be, with its successive consequences indefinitely instrumental to new satisfying events.[23]

As a matter of note, it may well be recalled that the instrumental character of consummatory experiences improves their quality in an additive way. Immediate appreciation of any perception is all the greater because of an understanding of how it was achieved and what it will now produce. Such understanding is the product of reflective inquiry into such experience as has been had. Dewey observes:

Possession and enjoyment of goods passes insensibly and inevitably into appraisal. First and immature experience is content simply to enjoy. But a brief course in experience enforces reflection; it requires but brief time to teach that some things sweet in the having are bitter in aftertaste and what they lead to. Primitive innocence does not last. Enjoyment ceases to be a datum and becomes a problem. As a problem, it implies intelligent inquiry into the conditions and consequences of a value-object; that is, criticism.[24]

What is sought in such inquiry is a grasp of "means-consequence" relations, an understanding of the "meanings" inherent in the situations in which the consummation occurs. For experimental inquirers such research is always pointed toward the possibility of management looking toward increased and improved values. It is admitted that "what cannot be understood cannot be managed intelligently," but the rationality of natural processes is held to be so universal as to warrant persistent and hopeful investigation looking toward competent manipulation. Even though the values may be of a refined intangible sort, their production is held to be manageable by intelligent control:

It is not a dream that it is possible to exercise some degree of regulation of the occurrence of enjoyments which are of value.[25]

It has been noted above that Dewey is definitely of the opinion that the principle of control, which has produced such beneficent results "in matters predominantly physical," should be carried over into the "psychophysical." Such control is naturally a matter of action "directed by knowledge" which is promoted not as an end in itself but as "method and means."

The aim and end is the securer, freer and more widely shared embodiment of values in experience by means of that active control of objects which knowledge alone makes possible.[26]

And thus certain experiences are deliberately induced and guided to serve as "instrumental efficacies" not for their own sake,

but for the sake of that full and more secure distribution of values which is impossible without instrumentalities.[27]

This discussion of the instrumental efficacy of consummatory experiences comprising an added significance has been set forth in general terms as being characteristic of all instruments. It is by so much valid in the religious experience of worship. The attainment of any perception of the relationships in which man's most precious values are achieved invariably occasions the joy of esthetic appreciation together with such added assurances and comforts as its efficacy as an instrumentality for the securing of such values generates in the mind. It is this joy which accounts for the zeal with which religious devotees engage in worship, and it is the unique instrumental efficacy of specific means involved which causes them to be held as sacred.

Despite the naive tendency to interpret the intense character of the joys experienced as being indicative of their absolute uniqueness, the course of repeated occurrences of such joys generates the inevitable appraisal and criticism which seeks to discover the means by which they can be had. Once such means are conceived they become the goal of deliberate effort, the aim of art in the endeavor to embody them in instrumentalities which can be manipulated at will. In the acquisition and employment of such mechanisms of control, intelligence is characteristically involved.

Practical skill, modes of effective technique, can be intelligently, non-mechanically *used* only when intelligence has played a part in their acquisition.[28]

The findings of men in their critical supervision of worship procedures have been commonly formulated as institutions of convention and custom which at first glance seem to lay restriction upon the spontaneity of the individual. But the discipline implied is of the very sort which was noted above to be the end of "all genuine education" and which is essential to accomplishments which in turn will satisfy man.

To view institutions as enemies of freedom, and all conventions as slaveries, is to deny the only means by which positive freedom in action can be secured.[29]

Here again the need for intelligence in construction and reconstruction of instruments which will engage and employ the environment is patently urgent.

Convention and custom are necessary to carrying forward impulse to any happy conclusion. A romantic return to nature and a freedom sought within the individual without regard to the exisiting environment finds its terminus in chaos . . . . Not convention but stupid and rigid convention is the foe.[30]

Religious worship is commonly carried on in procedures formulated in the social process and cherished in tradition. It is the mark of intelligence not to ignore or to discountenance such but to submit them to critical examination and to such reconstruction as then seems warranted. Dewey has expressed this idea in a comment which seems to reflect his characteristic idea of progress.

What is needed is intelligent examination of the consequences that are actually effected by inherited institutions and customs, in order that there may be intelligent consideration of the ways in which they are to be intentionally modified in behalf of generation of different consequences.[31]

The significance of intelligent reflection upon the effects resulting from the use of traditional instrumentalities can be clearly derived from this opinion of Dewey's without raising the question as to the validity of his surmise that "different consequences" are desired or needed. In the

event such consequences are the very value being sought, the bearing of intelligent research might well be toward understanding the technique of manipulation and improving the skills with which they are handled. In any case the function of intelligence is as beneficial in the understanding and improvement of this mode of human behavior as it is in any other.

The more common instrumentalities employed to promote worship experiences appearing in American culture have been developed within the framework of a theistic conception of the universe, in which the issues of the fortune, welfare, and destiny of man are held to be directly involved in his relationship to a personal Deity. Obviously the significance of any such general idea is grounded in the belief that such a Deity actually exists, that He actually will do what is ascribed to Him in this system of thought, and that any individual can actually enter into such a relationship with Him as will secure his eventual destiny to his complete satisfaction. When the individual in his own consciousness has felt the uncertainty of his own condition, status, and prospect so that he despaired of any favorable personal future whatever, and then perceives himself in a new relationship wherein the power of Deity will achieve for him a glorious "salvation," there follows exuberant triumphant joy that can well be designated "religious worship." This frame of belief in its broad systemic outline has a history that emerges from antiquity in the Hebrew tradition, is set forth in the literature commonly known as "The Old Testament Scriptures," and more latterly and more widely is being propagated in Christianity.

The remarkable vitality of this belief system in its capacity to reconstruct the conscious outlook and expectancy of the individual who commits himself in it, in its apparently universal fitness to reproduce its character-istic traits in any cultural circumstance of whatever time or place in history or society, and in its success in per-petuating and propagating itself throughout the historical vicissitudes of the Western world in the past three millennia or more, challenges scrutiny in any study of religious in-strumentalities. It belongs to experimental thinking to hold that the efficacy of any means is a function of the intelli-gence exercised in its constitution and employment. The weight of the testimony of history seems to indicate an intrinsic efficacy of whatever procedures have been em-ployed in the propagation of the Hebrew-Christian reli-gion. A comprehensive survey by description of all the devices employed will be neither practical nor necessary for the purpose in hand. An examination of some will suffice to demonstrate what may have been the operation of experimental intelligence in their construction and use.

The fact that the records[32] of antiquity focus major attention upon the pioneer work of Moses in the establish-ing of the pattern of culture known in history as "the reli-gion of Israel" challenges notice and examination of his work as an educator among his people. Apparently his pro-gram of education was undertaken at a crucial period in the history of his nation, and was markedly effective in structuring a distinctive system of belief and in grounding the pattern of a sustaining culture which has displayed extraordinary persistence in maintaining both its character and continuity. Through centuries of social change, wit-nessing the emergence, alteration, and disappearance of a motley variety of cultural phenomena, this Hebrew system and culture has persisted and propagated itself in ever widening range. A reasonable hypothesis from an experi-mentalist approach is that intelligent instrumentation was devised and employed.

Moses is not presented as appearing among his people as the founder of a unique culture but as a practical leader in a concrete actual situation which presented an unavoidable crisis. Living conditions were pictured as having become intolerable so that distress was acute. The sense of jeopardy would have been sharpened by the policy of oppression maintained in hostility by the dominant Egyptians, who apparently meant to destroy Israel. An old tradition which promised better things was intimated as lying dormant in the prevalent hopelessness and despair. The leadership of Moses was described as presenting the challenge of a new different possibility in another locale. The issue was presented in a proposal that the people migrate. This plan of action afforded a practical solution to the immediate problem set forth in the narrative and would be hailed as desirable by all because of its obvious benefits in their estimation. The religious quality was added by the dramatization of the ultimate import of the incident in the solemn rite of the slaying of the Passover Lamb. However, the requirement of their being dressed for the coming journey and their eating the roasted lamb by way of being prepared for the immediate actual outcome of the whole experience suggests experimental intelligence in leadership. The later dramatic escape through the windswept passageway across the Red Sea marshes where the Egyptian pursuers were mired and drowned would encourage the idea of their unique good fortune being directly related to the benevolent intervention of Divine Providence. Their jubilant exuberance pictured as grounded in this crucial deliverance was reported to have been directed into a celebration of victory, in which the meaning which Moses intended the people should retain in their minds was expressed poetically in Miriam's song of deliverance. Thus an instrumentality is presented as having been produced in the im-

mediate situation, which as an art product has continued to
serve effectively as a means of communicating to later
generations the religious significance of Israel's obedience
in following the guidance of Jehovah, as interpreted by
Moses in his role as prophet.

As effective as this incident may well have been in the
consciousness of Israel as described, its significance would
naturally have waned with the shifting of practical circumstances, the emergence of new problems, and the change in
personnel. Also the meaning of the event would have
changed in the course of ongoing experience. Thus the value
of the experience as a means to generate and to structure
a specific belief would have been lost. The institution of the
feast of the Passover as an annual commemoration of this
historic affair would appear to be an instrumentality of
experimental intelligence. The religious quality of this cere-
monial observance may well have been added by way of
dramatizing the ultimate import of the whole affair of being
delivered by the gracious intervention of the hand of God
in their affairs. However, the requirement as recorded of
their being dressed for the coming journey and their eating
the roasted lamb by way of being prepared for the immediate actual outcome of the whole experience has the flavor
of experimental intelligence at work. Sharing in the immediate pleasure of abundant food in festive atmosphere
would induce a measure of exuberant joy among a people
whose manner of life was meager enough at its best. This
natural spontaneous delight would then be caught up in the
stereotyped tradition of the meaning of the original event
and its ultimate import. Moses is represented as having
distinctly commanded that when the children in curiosity
inquired as to the meaning of this special celebration they
should be told the narrative of the exodus from Egypt. This
would have provided them with the "mind" to interpret

the institution of the Passover as having the same ultimate import as a symbol which the actual event was considered to have had.

The Christian celebration of the Lord's Supper is held traditionally to be in direct cultural descent from the Passover incident and commemoration. The facts as recorded, that the Last Supper was held on the eve of the Passover, that the Crucifixion took place on the day of the Passover feast, and that the Resurrection lends itself so patently as the counterpart of the Red Sea escape, would be empirical grounds for a direct transfer of traditional import to a new instrumentality. This it seems in actual occurrence to have been in marked fashion. All the pertinent meanings of the Passover which constitute the belief of Israel in a personal Deity who is held to design benevolent aid through direct intervention in response to committal in obedience to His revealed will have been incorporated in this new institution of the Lord's Supper. There is substitution of the affair of Calvary as the narrative which presents the "mind" to "understand" the commemorative rite, in the place of the exodus from Egypt. The eating has become largely symbolic, though in the early Christian communities it apparently continued in the proportions of a feast. Yet it is still eating and drinking. The intended import of its crucial significance as marking the beginning of something new and altogether different for all who participate in the committal to the will of God, therein dramatised, is the same. The Christian focus of attention upon the individual throughout the ceremony is a deviation in the pattern that seems to reflect some real difference in the belief being propagated.

The Christian rite of baptism is likewise an instrumentality designed to perpetuate in memory the significance of commencement in a way of life structured in the system of beliefs and practices, known as the Gospel. Though more obviously symbolic and therefore seeming more arbitrary, this ceremony maintains its meaning throughout the world as the distinctive sign of personal profession of acceptance of the Christian way of life as one's own. Diversity in mode of performance has tended to obscure the meaning of the rite in the life of the baptized, but actual participation in this overt behavior testifies the commitment of the neophyte to all that is involved in the proclamation of the evangelist. The meaning of the ceremony is now to be derived from the common understanding of its role in history. The solemnity of the administration of the sacrament together with the social consequences of participation combine to convey the intended import of the commencement of Christian living.

The counterpart of baptism in the Christian culture seems to have been circumcision in the culture of Israel. In some respects this rite would seem to have certain advantages as an instrumentality. There may have been a physical benefit which modern hygiene would understand, but which the Hebrew may well have recognized in the history of his people. There was a permanence in the result of this surgery that could never be hidden from the consciousness, nor from the notice of others. Then too the actual physical pain would serve to accent the sense of something real implied. However, there were limitations in that, being applicable only to males, it would tend to emphasize the lesser role of women in the life of the people.

The experimental intelligence exhibited in the selection of this rite as the distinctive sign of all who belonged in the group who were committed to live according to the revealed will of Jehovah becomes more and more apparent when the various practical implications of this particular physical surgery are noted. The actual physical mark left

on the flesh would imply something actual and real which it was being used to designate.

The belief system of Israel was constructed not only to emphasize the inception of a reorientation in personal affairs in the universe in terms of direct relationship with a personal Deity, but to recognize the constant bearing such relationship of obedience to the will of God would have upon daily practical concrete affairs. This phase of personal commitment was to be promoted through such instrumentalities as the Sabbath and the tithe

A break in routine activity and labor by cessation of work every seventh day seems to be obviously beneficial in the nature of things, being the testimony of objective observation from the standpoint of economy. Practices similar to this are instituted quite apart from any regard for tradition or religion. Letting the land lie fallow every seventh year would result in obvious agricultural benefits. Thus there was immediate practical advantage in observing the Sabbath as a period of rest.

The fact that physical labor tends to become drudgery when carried on continuously would constitute one day of rest in every seven days of living a time of relief, prompting gratitude and joy. Thus there was ample reason that the Israelite should note the Sabbath day with thankfulness and appreciation. It belonged to the formal instruction given in the law that this weekly holiday should be directly connected in their understanding of the will of God. It was to be observed in obedience, but understood as a blessing and a promise. Sometime in the future, the worshipper was led to believe, he would forever be entirely free from the curse of laboring to eke out physical existence "by the sweat of his face."

The actual observance of the practice was so directly involved in the practical economy of living, and any infraction could be so openly noted and publicly dealt with, that the effectiveness as an instrumentality to promote response seems readily understandable. The very fact that this observance would have an obvious direct bearing upon the outward public activities of all involved, and thus upon the socio-economic interests of the group, would augment the impression and stamp the significance in the consciousness of the participant. Thus the construing of this practice as an act of reverent worship, involving the eventual destiny in blessing from a benevolent appreciative Deity, produced an instrumentality exhibiting marked experimental intelligence.

The practice of giving the tithe of all income into the hands of the priests, who served as designated representatives of Deity, was also described as having been developed as an instrumentality to promote personal acceptance of the belief system taught by Moses, in which all physical benefits were to be taken as bounty direct from a living benevolent God. The fixing of a proportion "as the Lord has prospered," rather than an arbitrary standard assessment, would commend the whole practice as consistent with justice and equity, which were stated to be attributes of Jehovah, and would tend to emphasize the personal aspect of each individual response. The tribe of Levi was held to have been set apart in the society of Israel to attend to the elaborate program of ritual designed to induce religious response on the part of all the people. They were to be assigned no land upon which to make their living, but were designated to receive the tithes of the other twelve tribes. Obviously they would need to be sustained with food, clothing, shelter. Such supplies could come from those whom they served in their religious leadership in common justice as exchange of benefits. They would need the "tithe"; so that the giving of the tithe served an immediate practical

purpose. Thus there was the concrete aspect of the practice that served to ground its significance as an instrumentality in promoting belief in the whole interpretation of their relationship to God as set forth in the teachings of Moses.

The fact that this instrumentality was reported as being not as commonly employed as the Sabbath can be understood also from an experimental approach. Harvest came seldom. Some would have little direct responsibility for the disposition of the returns. The benefits of the priestly service of the Levites would not be so obvious. From an experimentalist point of view, the immediate benefits of giving the tithe being less obvious and the actual participation less general, the effectiveness as an instrumentality would be less. And such is precisely the testimony of the record. Apparently, as an instrumentality, giving the tithe would be effective whenever employed; but it would not be as popular nor as readily administered and therefore not as effective as the Sabbath.

Not all phases of religious experience can be so directly and obviously related to immediate practical benefits or results. All that is involved in the worship of God as a person, or the petitioning for His blessing in spoken request, which is commonly known as prayer, is so largely a matter of individual consciousness that its promotion presents a subtle problem in education. Here again experimental intelligence produces instrumentalities that facilitate control.

The practical problem involved in the control of worship as an experience in consciousness is lodged in the nature of religious experience. Any perception of the self as a unitary whole must hold in view the origin, infinite existential relationships, and destiny of the person as integrally related to the total universe. The only form in which the universe can be grasped for such perception is the ideal. The fact

that human experience involves overt physical contact behavior may complicate the problem of dealing with the
infinite, existential aspect of the self in the universe, but
at the same time it affords an opportunity of managing all
that concerns man. Dewey has remarked:

Lesser, more external fields of interaction are more manageable
than are wider and more intimate ones, and only through
managing the former can we direct the occurrence of the latter.[33]

And so it is that the physical elements in religious experience, while constituting a practical problem by their temporal and spatial limitations when related to that which is
ideal and infinite, at the same time become the handle by
which the whole may be managed.

Religious experience, by definition, acquires significance
and meaning by that which is distant, in that which is to
be had now only in imagination. While physical elements
are involved necessarily because of the nature of man, the
superior significance of the religious issues at stake demand
that the immediate bearing of the physical acts be con-
tained as far as possible. Dewey has pointed out:

When activity is directed by distant things, contact activities
must be inhibited or held in. They become instrumental; they
function only as far as is needed to direct the distance-conditioned activities.[34]

And so it follows that in the activities which generate
worship experiences, the physical things used are of the
nature of works of art, instrumentalities conceived and construed to facilitate production of desired results. Any such
art product is "a highly funded and generalized representation of the formal sources of ordinary emotional experience."
The form so represented was inherent in the total religious
experience of worship, was perceived in esthetic appreciation, and was embodied in structural form by creative art.

Form thus becomes the definitive element in the tool produced, to be used as an instrument in achieving repeatedly certain desired results.

This is illustrated in the case of public prayer as an instrumentality designed to induce and promote worship. Empirical data reveal that satisfying worship experiences have been had when prayer has been offered in a kneeling posture in unison with others in a public place specifically designated to be used for such practices. On the basis of this insight a form of praying is devised and produced to serve as a mode of procedure at the will of the devotees. The actual physical bending of the knees, the bowing of the head, the folding of the hands, the closing of the eyes, the modulated rhythmic recitation of the verbal utterances in solemn cadence, together with any and all other physical elements in the exercise, are unique and single in their occurrence. But the structure of the exercise, both internally in its practical arrangement and externally in all its meanings is an art product. It is an expression of the form of preparation for the worship experience as originally had and perceived, and then embodied in this formal prayer procedure. It is this form which gives to the physical elements involved their significance and worth. Because it was noted in reflection and embodied in an instrumentality designed to produce certain results, its effectiveness can be observed. Variant changes can be experimentally introduced, and improvement can be made in the search for maximum efficiency. In other words, experimental intelligence can function in the production and alteration of instrumentalities designed to promote the inner aspects of religious experience. The procedure in praying may be modified in changing circumstances as a result of experimental thinking.

The importance of implicating physical activity in such

instrumental procedures can be understood from an experimentalist approach. The practical benefit accruing from the use of such instrumentalities which order activities in forms which "carry" experiences of specific sorts to their "own integral fulfillment" is directly grounded in the actual articulation of the physical with the objective world. The immediate sense experience aroused by any activity tends to become first the dominant and then the only matter of significance. The deleterious effect this would have if unchecked in man's affairs is set forth by Dewey in these words:

Not only does the direct sense element—and emotion is a mode of sense—tend to absorb all ideational matter, but, apart from the special discipline enforced by physical apparatus, it subdues and digests all that is merely intellectual.[35]

Thus, in religious experience, the very fact that its unique and preeminent values are had in joy and satisfaction would point toward the eventual displacement of their distinctive meanings by an effervescent emotional significance. In so far as practical benefits are sought through religious experiences, it behooves any seeker for such goods to institute forms of procedure involving physical participation which will lead to actual consequences. Apparently such a course is both possible and desirable.

We can put ourselves or be put by others into situations where we are likely to have sensations and ideas in worthwhile ways, in ways that lead on to something else and so insure that the person be developed and recreated by them and not be exhausted by the mere having of them.[34]

It is not at all necessary that the person be aware, or that he understand precisely what is going on. The actual experience may manifest apparent spontaneity but the causal condition is operative nonetheless. Dewey points out

that "in this primary sense, then, the having of ideas is not so much something we do, as it is something that happens to us." Thus it would appear that the achieving of orderly competent thinking which will constitute worthy religious ideas and beliefs is grounded originally in orderly activity.

All people at the outset, and the majority of people probably all their lives, attain to some ordering of thought through ordering of action.[37]

The demands of experimental intelligence would result in a constant checking of the effectiveness of the instrumentality being employed. There would be occasional experimentation with novel features in procedures to note possible difference in results achieved. Better consequences would lead to changes in technique. In order that the worship experience might produce maximum values, practical activities designed to result in concrete benefits would be projected as a course of action to be followed in the release of the dynamic energy generated in the exhilaration of the joys of worship. Thus the worship would not only among other consequences give immediate pleasure, but in the obvious benefits accruing from subsequent conduct there would be enhanced satisfaction, as well as confirmed belief, strengthened conviction. Such eventual work programs will keep the worship experience wholesome within the larger frame of man's total being rather than permit dissipation in emotional self-indulgence, which would in the end undermine the potential values.

Despite the great importance thus ascribed to orderly practice, the physical activities so employed in procedural forms have no specific or occult significance in themselves. Unless their ulterior relationship is constantly recognized they will hinder rather than help in the project of inducing worship.

If the physical things used in teaching number or geography or anything else do not leave the mind illuminated with recognition of a *meaning* beyond themselves, the instruction that uses them is as abstruse as that which doles out ready-made definitions and rules, for it distracts attention from ideas to mere physical excitations.[38]

It belongs again to the intelligence operative in the construction of the instrumentality, in the form of the procedure embodied within the mechanism, that such intended reference shall be readily and consistently apparent. This was the purpose of their design and construuction.

All forms of artificial apparatus are intentional modifications of natural things so designed that they may serve better than in their natural state to indicate the hidden, the absent and the remote.[39]

This aim is achieved through the art involved in the production of the instrumentality. Thus the actual import is not a property of some intrinsic element but is in the consequences induced by the procedural structure employed. The direct bearing of this insight upon the promotion of the having of religious experience is set out clearly by Dewey in this illuminating passage:

But the influence that counted in the daily life of the mass of the people and gave them a sense of unity was constituted, it is safe to surmise, by sacraments, by song and pictures, by rite and ceremony, all having an esthetic strand, more than by any other one thing. Sculpture, painting, music, letters were found in the place where worship was performed. These objects and acts were much more than works of art to the worshipers who gathered in the temple. They were in all probability much less works of art to them than they are today to believers and unbelievers. But because of the esthetic strand, religious teachings were the more readily conveyed and their effect was the more lasting. By the art in them, they were changed from doctrines into living experiences.[40]

There can be no doubt that Dewey herein recognizes the instrumental efficacy of ritual in religious affairs.

The use of ritual practices as instrumentalities to initiate, guide, develop, sustain, and enhance religious experience in worship appears as a manifestation of experimental intelligence. The form of ritual is efficient to promote religious experiences because man is able to deal with the distant by the use of signs and to experience that which is beyond immediate grasp through symbols. Thus man can construct an immediate situation signifying the universe in its total bearing upon himself and so effect his own orientation to that which he esteems essential to the highest values of which he is aware. Also, in contemplation of that particular aspect of the universe he can induce within himself the resolution to adhere to that which he so esteems most precious. It is a matter of good fortune to man that through the exercise of experimental intelligence he can produce instrumentalities that will enable him so to manipulate his own experience as circumstance and interest may provide opportunity.

It was noted above that orderly physical activity was important in instrumentalities designed to induce worship experiences lest effervescent emotionalism dissipate and denature the intrinsic aim in the designed procedure. It remains now to be seen that an element of rationality must be included in order that the desired results may be secured. Religious experience involving much that is "absent" develops in consciousness generating beliefs which manifest certain "regular" intellectual aspects. "Creeds" may be taken to be formal verbal expressions of the "regular," "rational" character of the "beliefs" involved. As such they embody "consolidated meanings," refer to that which is absent or "transcendent," and partake of the fashion of all instrumentalities or "tools." Thus it can be expected that experimental intelligence will be operative in the construction and in the utilization of "creeds" as in any other mode of instrumentation.

In so far as activity has social aspects requiring mutual, cooperative, multiple acts in the course of any projected procedure, it is necessary that "tools," instrumentalities, have common acceptance as being held by everyone involved for what they portend. This requires that "meanings" be taken by "abstraction" from concrete examples and then formulated in verbal expressions, in which form they will be readily available for efficient application in the same sort of situations as those from which they were taken. This practical potentiality is recognized by Dewey:

To ascertain and state meanings in abstraction from social or shared situations is the only way in which the latter can be intelligently modified, extended and varied."

In order to be effective as an instrumentality the "meaning" embodied in the tool must be organically involved in the process that produces the results desired. This may well account both for the fact that great creeds have been forged in times of great heated controversy, and for the fact that each creed tends to be limited in the scope of its content by the specific issue generating the controversy which the creed was designed to end.

The prestige such an instrument may justly acquire by reason of its practical and "historic" effect may be very great, yet the "tool" is never anything more as such than instrumental to the having of ordinary experience. That classic "creeds" have attained great prestige and have become so technical in their meanings that only highly trained experts seem capable of understanding them is a matter of common note. It is salutary, though startling, to be reminded that no matter how intricate and highly

refined may be the shades of meaning set forth in the various statements of any creed, the creed itself as an instrumentality is never anything more than what it was designed to be, namely, a "representation" of "the formal sources of ordinary emotional experience." The prime significance of the creed is not derived from the specific matters dealt with in the credal statement but from the structure of the material set forth. Instrumental efficacy constitutes the nature and worth of a "creed" for experimentalist purposes, just as it would any other device designed to facilitate the reaching of certain ends. Though the language of description seems to point to the physical as being the primary field within which instrumentation operates, it by no means should be taken to disparage or discount the validity of instrumentalities in abstract and ideational areas. Dewey has observed:

If we follow the lead of empirically veifiable cases, it would then apear, that mathematical and moral essences may be dialectically fruitful, because like other machines they have been constructed for the purpose of securing certain consequences with the minimum of waste and the maximum of economy and efficiency."

The fact that ideational data are empirically real grounds the authenticity of intellectual instrumentalities designed to facilitate the production of certain results. This would suffice to establish any "creed" as an authentic instrumentality even though its character consists of its logical structure and its form is entirely verbal.

However, the ultimate educational significance of a creed" is not exhausted in its primary rational function. Dewey has insisted that "ideas are worthless except as they pass into actions which rearrange and reconstruct in some way, be it little or large, the world in which we live." So it follows that for religious ideas to have any didactic worth they must be geared to actual external situations. The function of a creed, while primarily manifested in the manipulation of ideas, is ultimately, by reason of the practical relationships of the ideas it orders, properly operative in the objective world of practical overt affairs. Because it is essentially an instrument, its actual validity is determined by the use which men make of it. Herein arises danger that the real function of the creed may be perverted.

The philosophic fallacy of holding instrumental characters to be final is particularly prone to develop in the matter of creeds. The significance of religious ideas is so great by reason of the paramount issues involved and because of their determinative bearing upon ideas of self-direction that their prestige, so grounded, suggests to the naive mind that they must have some intrinsic merit or quality which would justify esteeming them for their own sake. This soon develops a frame of mind that ignores the basic practical reference of the creed. Dewey has observed:

> Those who handle ideas through symbols as if they were things—for ideas *are* objects of thought—and trace their mutual relations in all kinds of intricate and unexpected relationships, are ready victims to thinking of these objects as if they had no sort of reference to things, to existence.
>
> In fact, the distinction is one between operations to be actually performed and possible operations as such, as merely possible."

Having thus conceived the creed to have intrinsic worth apart from overt and practical application, the mind of man tends to settle upon its form as fixed and inviolate, and to take pains to keep it unaltered. Such appears to be the testimony of history.

A statement that judgments about regulative ends and values, the creeds that are to govern conduct in its important in-

terests, are upon the whole matters of tradition, dogma and imposition from alleged authorities, hardly requires argument for its support."

The tendency of man to mistake the nature of a creed as an instrumentality must not be taken to imply that any such misunderstanding is necessary or inevitable. The operation of experimental intelligence will guard the mind of man from such a pitfall here as it does in other areas.

There is a simple practical condition which accounts for the notorious ease with which creeds are held in a sort of romantic idealism aloof from the practical affairs of life and in a kind of catatonic rigidity as being permanently settled in unalterable fixity. Dewey has pointed out that because they originate in a communal situation where they must be acceptable to each individual, they develop in the greatest possible abstraction.

In arriving at statements which hold for all possible experiences and observers under all possible varying individual circumstances we arrive at that which is most remote from any one concrete experience."

This fact of their characteristic abstraction renders creeds particularly susceptible to the inclusion of impractical unsound elements as speculation and vagary may suggest. The additional fact that their formulation is largely the work of creative intellection predisposes men to esteem and cherish them all the more fixedly and abitrarily. The primary safeguard against illusion in thought is the recurrent test which practical situations supply when ideas are put to work in overt experience. Just as those disciplines which deal with practical matters, such as engineering and medicine, tend to be the most sound because of such recurrent testing in actual concrete situations, so do the cogitations and reflections of belief, such as religious creeds, tend to be "erratic," extreme, impractical, because their practical application is obscure, tedious, and difficult. Despite their abstract character, experimental intelligence will function in their formulation, application, alteration, and revision to improve and to extend their instrumental efficacy. Dewey felt that it belongs to the residuum of classic philosophy that "creeds," "tenets," and "beliefs" have been so persistently held as unchangeable, and that an experimentalist approach to these matters would promote the operation of intelligence here, even as it followed the development of experimental inquiry in physical and material affairs. Referring to the benefits to be expected as a result of such a shift in philosophical outlook, he wrote:

With the transfer, these (standards, principles, rules) and all tenets and creeds about good and goods, would be recognized as hypotheses. Instead of being rigidly fixed, they would be treated as intellectual instruments to be tested and confirmed—and altered—through consequences effected by acting upon them. They would lose all pretense of finality—the ulterior source of dogmatism.[47]

Experimentalist thought will insist that the "form" of a creed be held tentatively as an instrumentality designed for a practical purpose,[48] and thus as subject to modification in intelligent revision on the basis of results produced by its use. But there is no ground here for the popular notion that creeds are to be discarded as being extraneous to and useless in actual religious experience. An experimental approach would indeed discount any "pretense of finality" as to form, but would in no sense jeopardize confidence in validity as to function. The "form" would be held tentatively but the "function" would be counted upon with even more assurance in view of experimental understanding of instrumental significance. The intelligent use of a creed as an instrumentality to

produce desired results will serve to avoid the historic proclivity to fixate loyalty to any specific form which may be developed.

Dewey has taken note that the historic attitude toward creeds has not been impressive in its manifestation of intelligence or sound judgment.

It is both astonishing and depressing that so much of the energy of mankind has gone into fighting for (with weapons of the flesh as well as the spirit) the truth of creeds, religious, moral and political, as distinct from what has gone into effort to try creeds by putting them to the test of acting upon them.[40]

Doubtless this comment served the purpose of Dewey's particular epistemological interest in that discussion of *The Quest for Certainty*, but in the face of the practical interest embodied in this discussion the situation as set forth by the two projects contrasted in this excerpt seems incomplete. The dominant experimentalist concern with creeds is not the matter of "form" but that of "function." The more fundamental alternative to "fighting for the truth of creeds" is that of striving for the realization of the consequences for which the creeds (in the experimentalist approach) would be designed as means, by an intelligent use of the creeds according to the purpose for which they are construed. The end of "creeds" is not "better creeds," but better conduct conducive to the making of better men and a better world. It will always be the aim of experimental intelligence to improve the means, the instrumentalities, the "art products," not for their own sake as ends in themselves, but for the sake of the increase and improvement of the goods being produced.

The analogy of a map to a creed is helpful toward a clear conception of the nature and function of creeds as instrumentalities in religious affairs. The map originates in the course of actual surveying, tediously and exhaustively carried out. Once formed, the map obviates the necessity of expensive repetition of tentative and investigative operations by recording the results which have been established. It will be the work of intelligence to check the accuracy of such findings from time to time and to strive for improvement as new methods and new instruments are developed to aid in more exact measurement. But the purpose of map making is not the making of maps. It is to facilitate such activities as travel, description and conveyance of property, planning operations of agriculture, mining, and such like. While it is to be noted that the better maps are produced under conditions where findings are checked and rechecked by intelligent interpretation of data supplied from their practical use, this is not the end of such effort toward improvement. Even so it is with creeds, within the experimentalist outlook. A creed is always a plan for living, for believing and doing. It is the formal product of rational reflection upon the procedures followed in arriving at certain desired consummatory experiences. Creeds are formulated in the matrix of conscious religious experience as structures of belief which set forth in literate form that which is to be followed if a specific consequence is sought. While constant revision is to be undertaken in the light of new data and better tools, there is a sense in which a practical limit in technical finesse may be approximated, at least in specific aspects of that which is being described. Shifting conditions, even in the interests and desires of the surveyors, may prompt recasting of such "maps," "plans," "formulae," "creeds." It is within the scope of experimental intelligence to function in such reconstruction even as it did in the initial formulation.

Creeds need not be lived out for a lifetime to provide data for such revision. By the use of symbols and the

processes of logical examination, the various significances can be discovered in reflection. Yet is must ever be kept in mind that the instrumental nature of the creed demands that an open-minded inductive observation of empirical results be the procedure followed rather than any rational deduction on the basis of any assumed "self-evident truths." This is to say, whereas the refined technical intellectual investigation of the significance of any creed will uncover many obscure and subtle aspects which would escape naive attention and thus promote alteration and improvement beyond the ken of the common mind, it is not to be expected that such sophisticated research will produce results upon which to reverse the general judgment of those who employ the creed. If the creed works in ordinary experience it is efficacious, and no amount of rationalizing interpretation can be expected to annul its validity. The tendency of some to discredit any creed on rational grounds, and who would propose the relegation of all creeds to some cultural junk pile as being judged outmoded and useless on the basis of logical analysis or philosophical premises, is simply neither sound nor intelligent from the experimental point of view. Actually the problem which creeds are designed to solve is not so much a matter of cognition as of volition. The end of religious belief and worship is not to know eternal truth absolutely but to commit the self to some aspect of the environing universe in expectant confidence wholeheartedly. While beliefs and creeds may be experimentally investigated in symbolic processes, they must be actually lived, or intended to be lived, in order to serve the purpose for which they were designed and constructed. In the light of these considerations the suitability of the pragmatic test to appraise validity, and of the exercise of experimental intelligence to increase efficiency and to facilitate maximum results, seems clearly apparent.[50]

The empirical origin of creeds has been alluded to and may be simply noted as the need for definitive verbalization of the meanings belonging to certain beliefs held in communal understanding. Controversy arising from difference of opinion causes tension and emotional strain which becomes intolerable and dangerous. In the ensuing intellectual debate contrary formulations of meaning are constructed by the disputants, while the attention of all is focused upon the task of settling upon some one statement of meaning that will be acceptable to the majority and so become the authorized view for all. Under tense circumstances of dramatic quality some formulation of expressed understanding is adopted. The immediate effect is one of intellectual clarification and of subsequent emotional release. This "creed' may now become the touchstone by which to identify and to certify the "Brethren." The result is one of satisfaction which enhances the worth of that formulation for those whose need has been served.

Such an origin would account for the esteem of the creed involved on the part of the group that had been disturbed. The later use of the creed as an authorized norm for the intellectual structure of the beliefs of succeeding generations in that continuing group would be a manifestation of the constant practical need in human consciousness of an adequate rationale to sustain deliberate adherence to a belief system. The changing circumstances in the normal course of human affairs would bring other phases of the belief system into focus for more specific interpretation. The mutations in language caused by novel events in human experience would make meanings unclear. Thus constant revision of formal utterance would be continually needed. Experimental intelligence could be employed to

advantage at all times in the rationalization process wherein preferred views, tenets, beliefs were being communicated and shared in the propagation of religious experience.

Throughout this examination of a number of well-known instrumentalities described as commonly employed in the promotion of religious experience, the operation of experimental intelligence has been noted as actual wherever improvement and increase of desired goods has been sought. It belongs to the function of philosophical reflection based upon an experimentalist approach to discover and to identify significant conditions or processes which operate causally to produce desired results. Such insight and understanding becomes then the means to ever more and better consequences. Thus the conclusion seems to be unavoidable that experimentalism applied to the problem of promoting the having of desired religious goods will result in benefits of improvement and increase in the results attained.

VII: CONCLUSION

Dewey's analysis of deliberate conduct recognizes an orderly sequence in the structure of conscious behavior, which has been taken to serve as the plan of this discussion. First, as man becomes aware of any particular phase of his experience he seeks through reflection to grasp the import for him in that situation in which he is involved. Such cognition is achieved by utilizing ideas, concepts, developed in past experience, so that the novel situation of which he has now become aware is recognized in terms of that with which he is familiar. Thus a basis for interpretation is laid in the very description with which the situation is defined and characterized in his own mind. His understanding of the meaning of the situation in terms of his own intellectual equipment will present the existential possibilities for him, so that he becomes aware of the potentialities of value confronting him and challenging him to intelligent conduct. This process of interpretation commonly leads to characterization of the situation in terms of the eventual values held to be obviously potential in the course of actual response. The first part of this treatise was developed as an exposition of processes in human experience which would provide a basis for understanding the operation of experimental intelligence in the course of religious experience.

The situation being thus "known" in terms of its practical possibilities, deliberation proceeds by projecting manipulation which will realize and distribute the potential values as efficiently as possible. Instrumentation

utilizes the knowledge procured in interpretation and devises tools, mechanisms, instruments, to facilitate the manipulation of events at will. With specific ends-in-view and a practical grasp of the nature of the situation in terms of familiar processes, the formulation of instrumental techniques is not only possible but becomes the obvious course for anyone who desires the best and the most for himself, and for his fellow men. This stage of instrumentation makes the greatest demand upon both intelligence and energy. It is at this point that decisive action is taken which determines the actual consequences as these will really occur, regardless of whatever existential possibilities there might have been. That Dewey himself should have focused his intellectual interest primarily at this point may be held as a proper token of his practical interest in the welfare and fortune of his fellow men. The second part of this discussion has been devoted to an analysis of several procedures commonly devised and employed as tools, instruments, to facilitate the having of cherished religious values, by way of understanding the role of experimental intelligence in the development of such procedures.

Enjoyment, suffering, delight, distress, pleasure, pain, satisfaction, aversion, and the like have been noted as constituting the spontaneous, unique, final consummatory "feeling" which highlights experience, gives significance and import to events, makes living tolerable or intolerable. Here is the ground of value, the source of all riches cherished by man. Despite the fleeting, fragile, unpredictable nature of such ineffable experiences they are prized above all else, esteemed precious in retrospect, and become the lodestar of aggressive effort. Identified as values in reflection, they challenge experimental research into the conditions and means of their occurrence in order that their realization, improvement, and distribution may be the aim of creative intelligence. It belongs to the empirical character of Dewey's thought to take values as they are given in the testimony of those who have them. The following comment about "beliefs" is indicative of his open attitude toward all "qualitative immediacies":

> Concerning beliefs and their objects taken in their immediacy "non-disputandum" holds, as truly as it does concerning tastes and their objects. If a man believes in ghosts, devils, miracles, fortunetellers, the immutable certainty of the existing economic regime, and the supreme merits of his political party and its leaders, he does so believe; they are immediate goods to him, precisely as some color and tones combinations are lovely, or the mistress of his heart is charming.[1]

The fact that Dewey implies a warning in this statement, as to the vagaries entertained by men in their "beliefs," must not jeopardize recognition of his full acceptance of the empirical validity of just such testimony. Not only does Dewey hold esthetic experiences as being entirely natural in their actual occurrence, but his consistent respect for empirical data leads him to find here an insight into the character of nature as a whole. This placing of "valuings" and "valueds" within nature has profound philosophical consequences. In the very nature of the case "immediacy of existence is ineffable," so that any direct consideration by an intellectual approach would be impossible; but Dewey's insight at this point brings esthetic final events within the scope of objective affairs where they can be studied and known. It has been the thesis of this discussion that when experimental analysis and interpretation are applied in the exposition of religious experience there will be neither reduction nor impairment of the values cherished by man, but rather an enlargement

and improvement of such values to the general advantage and benefit of all concerned.

When Dewey undertook to expound the philosophy of natural events on the basis of empirical data, he seemed to be guided by the impressive achievements and practical procedure of modern science. By defining nature as one interconnected universe, including every event as causally interrelated with all else that exists, the basis was laid for the application of science and the operation of experimental intelligence in any phase of human experience. As he proceeded to examine data presented in the testimony of mankind, Dewey developed his analysis and interpretation on the premise that experimental reflection is an indigenous mode of nature. Thus modern science is altogether natural in its principles. This natural role of science implies something profoundly significant from a practical point of view. It is the necessary condition, by whatever name it may be known, for the deliberate achievement of values. Dewey has pointed out in speaking of the function of philosophy:

It has to appraise values by taking cognizance of their causes and consequences; only by this straight and narrow path may it contribute to expansion and emancipation of values. For this reason the conclusions of science about matter-of-fact efficiencies of nature are its indispensable instruments. If its eventual concern is to render goods more coherent, more secure and more significant in appreciation, its road is the subject-matter of natural existence as science discovers and depicts it.

Only in verbal form is there anything novel in this conception of philosophy. It is a version of the old saying that philosophy is love of wisdom, of wisdom which is not knowledge and which nevertheless cannot be without knowledge. The need of an organon of criticism which uses knowledge of relations among events to appraise the casual, immediate goods that obtain among men is not a fact of philosophy, but of nature and life.[2]

When it is kept in mind that "nature" extends far beyond the physical, or the so-called material, so that the "matter-of-fact efficiencies of nature" about which "science" reaches "conclusions" will include conceptual, moral, ideal, cultural, and spiritual items, and that "science" is a mode of deliberate reflection applicable in any phase of consciousness, the potential role of science in promoting religious values can be understood. The novelty of utilizing science in the service of religion may be startling, but that such use is valid rests upon the whole structure of Dewey's thought. It is grounded in that view of nature and of man as a form of nature which comprises his whole philosophical outlook.

The actual function of science in the deliberate project to secure and distribute religious values would be involved in the recognition, interpretation, and manipulation of causal situations within which such values occur. Science is not directly concerned with the goods but with the means of production, possession, distribution, etc. Thus Dewey pointed out:

While "consciousness" as the conspicuous and vivid presence of immediate qualities and of meanings, is alone of direct worth, things not immediately present, whose intrinsic qualities are not directly had, are primary from the standpoint of control. For just because the things that are directly had are both precious and evanescent, the only thing that can be thought of is the conditions under which they are had.[3]

When it is kept in mind that religious values are "qualitative immediacies" occurring in "consciousness," the basic discrimination between religious objects and scientific objects is readily apparent, and the secondary, contributory, instrumental character of scientific objects is likewise

obvious. When this fact is kept in view, that scientific "reflection is concerned with the order which conditions, prevents, and secures" the occurrence of primary, consummatory, final qualitative events, the practical relationship which could be intelligently maintained between "science" and "religion" is apparent.

Granted that human beings have religious values and that in the course of history certain procedures have been developed in which man seeks the recurrence and the sharing of such consummatory experiences, science would take such "instrumental efficiencies" and through analytic experimental reflection acquire knowledge of the causal relations involved so that the part played by man himself might become more efficient and more readily controlled. At this point scientific methods approximate the character of art, but do not in any way jeopardize the occurrence and the realization of religious values. It would be within the scope of empirical naturalism to accept the testimony of history as to the practical import of naive techniques employed in the promotion of religious experience. It would be within the province of experimental reflection to examine such procedures by way of identifying what was intrinsically involved in the having of the values sought, and constructing better instruments to accomplish the end-in-view more economically and more widely. The propriety of utilizing the method of science for the purpose of improving and extending the propagation of the Christian religion is obvious at this point.

The extension of experimental inquiry into the problem of achieving religious goods will contribute to their improvement both in making them more accessible in deliberate effort, and in refining them by freeing them from extraneous and useless accretions of a cultural, traditional, or philosophical sort.

Dewey distinguishes "immediate goods casually occur-ring," and "immediate goods which have been reflectively determined," and holds the latter to be better than the former. The very fact that their occurrence can be antici-pated, secured, prolonged, together with the additional elation of triumph whenever such aim is achieved, aug-ments and extends the enjoyment experienced.

However, the nature of the additive significance im-parted by reflection to any "good" seems to consist pri-marily of knowledge of "properties and relations" of causal import. Apparently this provides a criterion for appraisal and a guidance for realization. Dewey has noted:

> The all-important matter is what lies back of and causes ac-ceptance and rejection; whether or not there is method of dis-crimination and assessment which makes a difference in what is assented to and denied. Properties and relations that *entitle* an object to be found good in belief are extraneous to the qualities that are its immediate good; they are causal, and hence found only by search into the antecedent and eventual.[4]

This observation is of unusual significance in the field of religious experience, inasmuch as the belief objects involved in religious values are so often suspect because of their ineffable elements. Anything that could be desig-nated "mystic" in origin is commonly held as notoriously irrational to such degree that the whole class of beliefs known as religious has been suspected as having no signifi-cant validity. The above quotation shows that, whereas such suspicion might well be directed to "beliefs," "goods," or "values" which are had blindly and are cherished with-out reflection, there would be no justification for such wholesale discard of beliefs that have been "reflectively determined" by inquiry into "antecedent and eventual" con-ditions.

This appraisal of belief objects or goods, which would

indicate that validity depends upon empirical possession and critical inquiry along scientific lines, can be extended further to note that:

Poetic meanings, moral meanings, a large part of the goods of life are matters of richness and freedom of meanings, rather than of truth; a large part of our life is carried on in a realm of meanings to which truth and falsity as such are irrelevant.[5]

It need imply no malice to observe that this comment relieves the person cherishing religious doctrines and values from the necessity of refuting skeptical heckling as to the verifiability of all contents in what is believed. Doubtless no one holding real conviction as to spiritual existences would ever consider such an intellectual position as adequate for his own thinking, but it seems proper to note that in the experimental approach empirical data are acceptable without recourse to historical proof or logical demonstration. The authenticity of a religious value is grounded in several empirical conditions. That "imaginary," "visionary," "untrue" elements might be included in religious goods is to be admitted as possible, as it is actually patent in the public religious beliefs and claims put forth among men. While experimental thinking as set forth by Dewey must needs allow for such vagaries, it will follow in the application of critical intelligence that certain methods of examination, verification, experimentation, and revision will be useful in the refinement of such beliefs toward ever increasing validity and authenticity. It has been the thesis of this discussion that the exercise of intelligent criticism in the field of religious experience will be as beneficial in the attainment of cherished goods as it has manifested itself to be in other areas of human interest.

Despite the additive significance of the operation of instrumental intelligence in the process of having religious experience, it has been noted that the whole project of the achieving of such values is grounded in original satisfactions, pleasures, and contentments occurring in the course of living. The fact that such initial enjoyments may have been experienced in naive fashion, may have been inaccurately described and mistakenly interpreted, does not lessen their primary import. Enough that they were had, appreciated, and taken to be desirable. Thus they were "valued," and so became "goods" to be sought, cherished, and shared. Dewey has expresed this fact succinctly when he stated:

Consummations have first to be hit upon spontaneously and accidentally—as the baby gets food and all of us are warmed by the sun—before they can be objects of foresight, invention and industry.[*]

However, the having of such spontaneous consummatory experiences does not lead directly into the institution of procedures designed to produce, improve, and distribute such results. The history of mankind records the fact that men have enjoyed, appreciated, and cherished values without undertaking to achieve them by intelligent manipulation of causal conditions. Their occurrence has been left frequently to chance with a resultant occult character in their manifestation. It has been noted that the contribution of experimental intelligence to the achievement of such values is that it becomes a matter of deliberate procedure undertaken in confident expectation of known consequences. It is when perceived causal relations are embodied in art products as instrumentalities designed to achieve specific results that such procedures can be controlled.

Art is the sole alternative to luck; and divorce from each other of the meaning and value of instrumentalities and ends is the

essence of luck. The esoteric character of culture and the supernatural quality of religion are both expressions of this divorce.[7]

There need be no concern that the introduction of deliberate procedures of experimental intelligence will impair the quality of the religious experiences so promoted, on the general premise that whatever is naively and spontaneously natural is more likely to be authentic. Such premise has been seen to be fallacious.

The goods of art are not less good in their goodness than the gifts of nature; while in addition they are such as to bring with themslves open-eyed confidence. They are the fruit of means consciously employed; fulfillments whose further consequences are secured by conscious control of the casual conditions which enter into them.[8]

The distinction between "art" and "nature" is helpful to clearer understanding of the point at issue.

In other words, art is not nature, but is nature transformed by entering into new relationships where it evokes a new emotional response.[9]

Just as "art" is thus seen to be a particular construction of "nature," it could be noted that "religion" is construed out of the "religious." The "religious" is natural, whereas "religion" is artistic with all the advantages and liabilities inherent therein. To recognize that education in religion, because it makes deliberate purposeful use of instrumentalities, may manifest the "artificial," may support the conclusion that it should never be held as "final" in form. But it does not at all imply that it is to be considered as being either invalid or incorrigible. As a matter of fact it is just the element of art involved that gives promise of possible development of efficiency and practical significance in this activity in human consciousness.

This exposition of the occurrence of the having of religious goods in the terms of Dewey's experimentalist analysis of experience not only demonstrates the structure of the events involved but points to the possibility of improving and controlling this mode of human behavior. Apparently the production of religious goods can be deliberately controlled by the use of intelligent procedures in the course of which effective instrumentalities may be constructed and employed to advantage. The design and use of such "tools" will be conceived, developed, and improved by the continued application of experimental intelligence. The preceding discussion warrants several practical judgments which can be taken as directives in any plan designed to promote the achieving and the sharing of religious goods.

An experimentalist approach to the problem of securing religious goods would begin by noting that such goods are actually had according to the empirical testimony of human history. Observation of the situations in which such goods are reported to have occurred will then be made in an effort to discover antecedent-consequent conditions. This study will be continued until some organic environmental, overt participation is identified as means in the causal sequence leading to the end-in-view. The practical obvious relation between means and the end-in-view is the basis for judgments pertaining to the efficacy of procedures employed. With attention now focused upon "means" and upon "consequences" as they actually occur when specific means are employed, observation of empirical events provides data for progressive revision and alteration of procedures with the aim of securing more and better results. In the course of such exercise of experimental intelligence some implications of the philosophy

of John Dewey for education in religion will be demonstrated.

In the light of the foregoing discussion the following practical expectations seem to be warranted in the course of deliberate promotion of religious experience when experimental intelligence as set forth by Dewey is employed.

1. Religious goods will be taken as authentic and real upon the testimony of those who claim to have had them. History, biography, individual report, and social consequence will supply evidence for data in the study of religion. Occurring in human experience, such goods will be held as natural in their origin and development. They will be considered as events having antecedents and consequences, so that their occurrence can be observed, considered, and understood. Philosophic reflection will recognize the means for their production and the results of their actualization. Deliberate intellectualization of processes involved, with objective abstractions of regular sequential relations, will be undertaken with the aim of discovering the structure of causal conditions in order that instrumentation may be devised to ensure the future occurrence, increase, and betterment of such goods. Not the denial but the achievement, the improvement, and the distribution of these values will belong to the operation of experimental intelligence.

2. Religious experiences producing desired goods will be held to involve regular organic environmental interactions which can be identified and observed. Reflection to discover relations between practical affairs which could be managed, and ideal features which cannot be handled, will be pursued to perceive what public procedures might be expected to result in the desired goods. The patterns of such procedures would be looked for in the course of experience producing these values. Experimentalist under-

standing will avoid the fallacy of taking such instrumental aspects as having final significance. Also the process of reflection will not be concluded as though an absolute understanding had been reached. There will be constant attention to note new evidence, review of matters already considered, and continuous reflection upon such insights already had, with a view to better understanding. An attitude of critical appraisal will be maintained in alert vigilance with the aim to achieve better understanding of how such goods might be secured in more quantity and better quality.

3. The perception of the pattern of antecedent conditions which have been observed to produce desired consequences in consummatory values will stimulate the conceiving of some form of procedure which can be expected to produce such conditions. In order to secure ready and repeated use of such procedure, experimental intelligence will seek the incorporation of certain events which have been known to give immediate pleasure or practical benefit. Thus participation in the total procedure may be expected by individuals who have interest in the immediate obvious benefits but who may be unaware of the greater eventual consequences which will follow. Likewise these artful procedures designed to lead into the having of desired religious consummatory experience will be geared into concrete situations of actual need in such a way that practical results of the betterment of human affairs will occur. Thus the continued use of such instrumentalities will be secured in the knowledge and consent of persons who have concern for the common fortune and welfare of mankind. A deliberate program to secure consistent and continued use of specific procedures will become a social institution, and thus a part of the prevailing culture.

4. Inasmuch as the procedures so devised will be under-

stood as instrumental, designed to be effectual in production of specific results, they will not be taken as final or inviolate. They will be kept under constant observation in their operation, and held subject to revision at any time when results seem to indicate some alteration might be to advantage. Variations in response will be noted as indices of need or opportunity for revision. The basic problem, the accepted interpretation, and the approved plan of action will be continually reviewed from the shifting point of view, the changing interest, and the new insights which are always modifying the approach of thinking persons. New hypotheses, creative ideas, will produce inventions of novel devices in procedure. Experimentation and careful verification of efficiency will lead to changes in accepted procedure. In all this the tendency in social inertia to establish stereotyped patterns as matters of permanent tradition, and to fixate certain routines as sacred, together with other aspects of cultural lag, will be overcome by this function of experimental intelligence operating in individual mind.

5. Experimental understanding will recognize that a phase of the utility of any procedure is its acceptability to those who are to possess the desired goods. Social approval can be grounded partly in cultural continuity. The testimony of the past will be regarded, and incorporated with the experimental and empirical data, as the basis for confident adoption of specific techniques. At the same time the recognition of constant change in the world will point to inevitable need for change in procedure. Thus experimental intelligence will guide toward not supersession but reconstruction of existing procedures. Religious exercises of any sort will be taken as significant for whatever goods were ever attained as a result of their use, but will be examined in light of better understanding and because of changed circumstances that extraneous elements not now of any func-

tional value, and cultural accretions which actually impair validity, may be eliminated. At the same time there will be constant searching for more economic, more efficient techniques which can be seen as improvements to the having of more and better goods.

6. Experimental understanding will recognize also that for instrumentalities designed to promote religious experience to be kept wholesome, they must lead into actions that will benefit the gross concrete experience of mankind. The proclivity of man to indulge in moments of ecstasy occurring in the course of daydreaming, fancy, and wishful thinking will be checked by the demands of experimental intelligence that insist that all thinking be grounded in the administration of practical organic environmental interactions involving the life of the human organism in its total relationships. It will belong to the function of experimentalist reflection to keep the ultimate destiny of the self and the proximate situation of the organism in one perspective. This will mean discipline of immediate experience in the interest of eventual benefits of concrete tangible sort. In the same way individual preference will be subjected to the requirements of social approval, since the greater values are had in the relationship of the self with others.

7. One general conclusion seems warranted that seems to promise untold benefit for mankind. Experimental intelligence will not aim to discount, discredit, or deny the goods which are reported as had in religious experience. On the contrary, deliberate effort will be undertaken to secure the occurrence of more and better goods at will. Their occurrence will be increased by the construction and use of better instrumentalities which will facilitate the deliberate management of the means for their production. Their quality will be improved both because their nature will be better understood and because they will have been sub-

jected to critical revision in the light of careful review and examination. Apparently there is no reason to question that religious experience can be initiated, guided, promoted, enriched, and shared by the operation of experimental intelligence in the construction and employment of suitable educational techniques in the use of instrumentalities or procedures designed for that purpose.

NOTES

I: INTRODUCTION

1. John Dewey, *Problems of Men* (New York: Philosophical Library, 1946), pp. 11-12.

2. *Ibid.*, pp. 10-11.   3. *Ibid.*, p. 11.

4. Paul Arthur Schilpp (ed.), *The Philosophy of John Dewey* (Evanston and Chicago: Northwestern University, 1939), p. 594.

5. *Ibid.*, pp. 93-94.

II: THE PHILOSOPHY OF JOHN DEWEY

1. However, for Dewey, human intelligence involves the use of symbols found only on the *social* level. (See *Logic* [New York: Henry Holt and Company, 1938], pp. 43-44.)

2. Anent this possibility Dewey has a passage in *Experience and Nature* (New York: W. W. Norton & Co., Inc., 1929), pp. 33-35, that elaborates upon its significance.

III: THE OPERATION OF INTELLIGENCE

1. John Dewey, *Philosophy and Civilization* (New York: Minton, Balch & Co., 1931), p. 78.

2. *Ibid.*, p. 86.   3. *Ibid.*, p. 88.

4. *Ibid.*, p. 92.

5. John Dewey, *How We Think* (Boston: D. C. Heath & Co., 1910), pp. 190-94.

6. John Dewey, *The Quest for Certainty* (New York: Minton, Balch & Co., 1929), p. 113.

7. *Ibid.*, p. 258.

8. John Dewey, *Problems of Men* (New York: Philosophical Library, 1946), p. 20.

9. John Dewey, *Experience and Nature* (New York: W. W. Norton & Co., Inc., 1929), pp. 43-44.

10. Dewey, *The Quest for Certainty*, p. 302.

11. *Ibid.*, p. 306.

12. Dewey, *Experience and Nature*, p. 75.

13. *Ibid.*, pp. 131-132.

14. *Ibid.*, p. 101.

15. *Ibid.*, p. 116.

16. *Ibid.*, pp. 262-63.

17. *Ibid.*, pp. 421-22.   18. *Ibid.*, p. 422.

19. Dewey, *The Quest for Certainty*, pp. 214-15.

20. Dewey, *Experience and Nature*, p. 13.

21. *Ibid.*

22. John Dewey, *Art as Experience* (New York: Minton, Balch & Co., 1934), p. 333.

23. *Ibid.*, p. 345.

24. *Ibid.*, p. 246.

25. John Dewey, *How We Think* (new ed.; Boston: D. C. Heath & Co., 1933), p. 202.

26. Dewey, *Art as Experience*, pp. 35-36.

27. *Ibid.*, p. 37.

28. *Ibid.*, pp. 43-44.   29. *Ibid.*, p. 44.

30. Dewey, *Experience and Nature*, p. 232.

31. Dewey, *Art as Experience*, p. 104

32. Dewey, *Experience and Nature*, p. 270.

33. *Ibid.*, p. 182.   34. *Ibid.*, p. 428.

35. Dewey, *The Quest for Certainty*, p. 272.

36. *Ibid.*, p. 234.   37. *Ibid.*, p. 236.

38. Dewey, *Experience and Nature*, p. 237.

39. Dewey, *How We Think* (1933 ed.), p. 101.

40. Dewey, *The Quest for Certainty*, p. 232.

41. *Ibid.*, p. 244.   42. *Ibid.*, p. 189.

43. Dewey, *Experience and Nature*, pp. 200-201.

44. John Dewey, *Human Nature and Conduct* (New York: Henry Holt and Company, 1922), pp. 216-17.

45. Dewey, *How We Think* (1933 ed.), p. 21.

46. *Ibid.*, p. 118.

47. Dewey, *The Quest for Certainty*, p. 107.

48. *Ibid.*, p. 123.

49. Dewey, *How We Think* (1933 ed.), p. 18.

50. Dewey, *The Quest for Certainty*, p. 138.

51. *Ibid.*, p. 168.

52. Dewey, *How We Think* (1933 ed.), p. 99.

53. *Ibid.*, p. 73.   54. *Ibid.*, p. 99.

55. Dewey, *Experience and Nature*, pp. 158-59.

56. Dewey, *The Quest for Certainty*, p. 214.

57. Dewey, *Human Nature and Conduct*, p. 314.

58. Dewey, *The Quest for Certainty*, p. 213.

59. Dewey, *Human Nature and Conduct*, pp. 245-55.

60. Dewey, *Art as Experience*, p. 44.

61. Dewey, *Experience and Nature*, pp. 296-97.

62. *Ibid.*, p. 317.

63. Dewey, *How We Think* (1933 ed.), p. 286.

64. Dewey, *The Quest for Certainty*, p. 136.

65. Dewey, *Human Nature and Conduct*, pp. 205-6.

66. *Ibid.*, p. 267.   67. *Ibid.*, p. 238.

68. *Ibid.*, p. 299.   69. *Ibid.*, p. 269.

70. Dewey, *The Quest for Certainty*, p. 250.

IV: THE NATURE OF MAN

1. John Dewey, *Experience and Nature* (New York: W. W. Norton & Co., Inc., 1929), p. 418

2. *Ibid.*, p. 434.

3. *Ibid.*, p. 258.

4. John Dewey, *The Quest for Certainty* (New York: Minton, Balch & Co., 1929), p. 225.

5. John Dewey, *Art as Experience* (New York: Minton, Balch & Co., 1934), p. 263.

6. Dewey, *Experience and Nature*, p. 219.

7. *Ibid.*, p. 307.

8. John Dewey, *How We Think* (Boston: D. C. Heath & Co., 1910), p. 43.

9. Dewey, *Experience and Nature*, p. 305.

10. *Ibid.*, p. 300.

11. Dewey, *Art as Experience*, pp. 72-73.

12. Dewey, *The Quest for Certainty*, p. 232.

13. Dewey, *Art as Experience*, p. 73.

14. Dewey, *Experience and Nature*, p. 90.

15. *Ibid.*, p. 294.   16. *Ibid.*, p. 246.

17. *Ibid.*, p. 256.   18. *Ibid.*

19. Dewey, *Art as Experience*, pp. 281-82.

20. Dewey, *Experience and Nature*, p. 70.

21. *Ibid.*   22. *Ibid.*, p. 71.   23. *Ibid.*, p. 86.

24. *Ibid.*, p. 235.   25. *Ibid.*, p. 73.   26. *Ibid.*

27. *Ibid.*, p. 90.   28. *Ibid.*, p. 74.   29. *Ibid.*

30. *Ibid.*   31. *Ibid.*, p. 151.   32. *Ibid.*, p. 349.

33. *Ibid.*, p. 350.

34. Dewey, *Art as Experience*, p. 246.

35. Dewey, *The Quest for Certainty*, p. 281.

36. John Dewey, *Human Nature and Conduct* (New York: Henry Holt and Company, 1922), p. 137.

37. *Ibid.*, p. 138.

38. Dewey, *Experience and Nature*, p. 219.

39. *Ibid*, p. 233   40. *Ibid.*

41. Dewey, *Art as Experience*, p. 264.

42. Dewey, *Experience and Nature*, p. 185.

43. *Ibid.*, p. 122.   44. *Ibid.*, p. 136.

45. *Ibid.*, p. 163.   46. *Ibid.*, p. 247.

47. *Ibid.*, p. 245.

48. Dewey, *The Quest for Certainty*, p. 247.

49. Dewey, *Art as Experience*, p. 333.

50. Dewey, *Experience and Nature*, p. 175.

51. *Ibid.*, p. 280.   52. *Ibid.*, p. 166.

53. *Ibid.*, p. 167.

54. Dewey, *The Quest for Certainty*.

55. *Ibid.*, p. 125.

56. Dewey, *Experience and Nature*, p. 179.

57. Dewey, *Art as Experience*, p. 28.

58. Dewey, *Human Nature and Conduct*, pp. 16-17.

59. *Ibid.*, p. 314.   60. *Ibid.*, pp. 314-15.

61. Dewey, *Experience and Nature*, p. 202

62. Dewey, *Art as Experience*, pp. 334-35.

63. Dewey, *Experience and Nature*, pp. 178-79.

64. *Ibid.*, p. 179.

65. Dewey, *Art as Experience*, p. 336.

66. Dewey, *Human Nature and Conduct*, p. 331.

67. Dewey, *Art as Experience*, p. 244.

68. Dewey, *Human Nature and Conduct*, pp. 316-17.

69. Dewey, *Experience and Nature*, p. 347.

70. Dewey, *How We Think*, p. 59.

71. Dewey, *Experience and Nature*, p. 322.

72. *Ibid.*, p. 270.

73. Dewey, *The Quest for Certainty*, p. 18.

74. Dewey, *Art as Experience*, p. 270.

75. Dewey, *Experience and Nature*, p. 233.

76. Dewey, *The Quest for Certainty*, p. 277.

77. *Ibid.*, p. 299.

78. Dewey, *How We Think*, p. 256.

79. *Ibid.*, p. 24.   80. *Ibid.*, pp. 28-29.

81. *Ibid.*, p. 32.

82. Dewey, *Art as Experience*, p. 300.

83. Dewey, *The Quest for Certainty*, pp. 227-28.

84. *Ibid.*, p. 228.

85. Dewey, *How We Think*, p. 23.

86. *Ibid.*, p. 97.

87. Dewey, *Experience and Nature*, p. 339.

88. Dewey, *How We Think*, p. 136.

89. Dewey, *Human Nature and Conduct*, p. 329.

90. Dewey, *Experience and Nature*, p. 405.

91. *ibid.*

92. Dewey, *The Quest for Certainty*, p. 268.

93. Dewey, *Experience and Nature*, p. 396.

94. Dewey, *The Quest for Certainty*, p. 264.

95. *Ibid.*, p. 262.   96. *Ibid.*, p. 268

97. *Ibid.*, p. 299.   98. *Ibid.*, p. 35.

99. *Ibid.*, p. 36.

100. John Dewey and James H. Tufts, *Ethics* (New York: Henry Holt and Company, 1908), p. 295.

101. Dewey, *Experience and Nature*, p. 399.

102. Dewey, *The Quest for Certainty*, p. 262.

103. John Dewey, *Problems of Men* (New York: Philosophical Library, 1946), p. 8.

104. *Ibid.*, pp. 11-12.   105. *Ibid.*, p. 27.

106. *Ibid.*, p. 31.

107. Dewey, *Experience and Nature*, p. 284.

108. *Ibid.*, p. 272.

109. Dewey, *Art as Experience*, p. 240.

110. *Ibid.*, p. 330.

111. *Ibid.*, p. 336.   112. *Ibid.*, p. 332.

113. *Ibid.*, p. 326.   114. *Ibid.*, p. 345.

115. *Ibid.*, p. 265.   116. *Ibid.*, pp. 344-45.

117. Dewey, *Experience and Nature*, pp. 301-2.

118. *Ibid.*   119. *Ibid.*, p. 82.

V: THE MEANING OF RELIGION

1. John Dewey, *Experience and Nature* (New York: W. W. Norton & Co., Inc., 1929), p. 128.

2. *Ibid.*, pp. 69-70.

3. John Dewey, *Human Nature and Conduct* (New York: Henry Holt and Company, 1922), pp. 26-27.

4. It is the logical dependence of Dewey's system of thought upon this existential trait in Nature that moves Prof. Childs to insist that, despite his avowal to the contrary, Dewey does have definite metaphysical elements in his conceptions.

5. Dewey, *Experience and Nature*, p. 86.

6. *Ibid.*, p. 131.   7. *Ibid.*, p. 133.

8. John Dewey, *The Quest for Certainty* (New York: Minton, Balch & Co., 1929), p. 135.

9. *Ibid.*, pp. 135-36.

10. *Ibid.*, p. 133.   11. *Ibid.*, p. 248.

12. Dewey, *Experience and Nature*, p. 128.

13. Dewey, *The Quest for Certainty*, p. 104.

14. *Ibid.*, pp. 221-22.   15. *Ibid.*, p. 249.

16. Dewey, *Experience and Nature*, p. 110.

17. *Ibid.*, p. 58.   18. *Ibid.*, pp. 151-52.

19. *Ibid.*, p. 161.   20. *Ibid.*, p. 163.

21. *Ibid.*, p. 165.   22. *Ibid.*, p. 317.

23. Dewey, *The Quest for Certainty*, p. 312.

24. John Dewey, *Art as Experience* (New York: Minton, Balch & Co., 1934), p. 15.

25. Dewey, *Experience and Nature*, p. 80.

26. Dewey, *The Quest for Certainty*, p. 235.

27. Dewey, *Experience and Nature*, p. 108.

28. Dewey, *Art as Experience*, p. 120,

29. *Ibid.*, p. 194.   30. *Ibid.*, p. 165.

31. Dewey, *Experience and Nature*, p. 391.

32. Dewey, *Art as Experience*, p. 137.

33. *Ibid.*, pp. 50-51.   34. *Ibid.*, p. 107.

35. *Ibid.*, p. 201.   36. *Ibid.*, p. 176.

37. *Ibid.*, p. 297.

38. Dewey, *Experience and Nature*, p. 359.

39. *Ibid.*, p. 365.

40. Dewey, *Art as Experience*, p. 62.

41. Dewey, *Experience and Nature*, pp. 369-70.

42. *Ibid.*, p. 389.   43. *Ibid.*, p. 372.

44. Dewey, *Art as Experience*, p. 26.

45. *Ibid.*, p. 329.   46. *Ibid.*, p. 268.

47. *Ibid.*, p. 189.   48. *Ibid.*, p. 348.

49. Dewey, *Experience and Nature*, p. 432.

50. Dewey, *Art as Experience*, p. 105.

51. *Ibid.*, p. 286.   52. *Ibid.*, p. 270.

53. *Ibid.*, p. 271.   54. *Ibid.*, p. 329.

55. *Ibid.*, p. 347.

56. Dewey, *Experience and Nature*, pp. 41-42.

57. Dewey, *The Quest for Certainty*, p. 10.

58. *Ibid.*, p. 292.   59. *Ibid.*, pp. 14-16.

60. Dewey, *Human Nature and Conduct*, p. 318.

61. Dewey, *The Quest for Certainty*, p. 307.

62. *Ibid.*   63. *Ibid.*, p. 308.

64. Dewey, *Art as Experience*, p. 19.

65. Dewey, *Human Nature and Conduct*, pp. 263-64.

66. Dewey, *Art as Experience*, p. 18.

67. Dewey, *Human Nature and Conduct*, p. 330.

68. *Ibid.*, pp. 331-32.   69. *Ibid.*, p. 264.

70. *Ibid.*, p. 331.   71. *Ibid.*, pp. 216-17.

72. *Ibid.*, p. 331.

73. Dewey, *Art as Experience*, p. 17.

74. *Ibid.*

75. Dewey, *The Quest for Certainty*, p. 303.

76. *Ibid.*, p. 306.   77. *Ibid.*, p. 304.

78. Dewey, *Human Nature and Conduct*, p. 263.

79. Dewey, *The Quest for Certainty*, p. 235.

80. Dewey, *Human Nature and Conduct*, p. 225.

81. *Ibid.*, p. 120.

82. Dewey, *Experience and Nature*, p. 420.

83. *Ibid.*, p. 426.

84. Dewey, *The Quest for Certainty*, p. 255.

85. *Ibid.*, p. 252.

86. Dewey, *Human Nature and Conduct*, p. 279.

87. Dewey, *Experience and Nature*, p. 317.

88. Dewey, *Human Nature and Conduct*, pp. 280-81.

89. Dewey, *The Quest for Certainty*, p. 138.

90. *Ibid.*, p. 268.   91. *Ibid.*, p. 270.

92. Dewey, *Experience and Nature*, p. 376.

93. Dewey, *Human Nature and Conduct*, p. 293.

94. John Dewey and James H. Tufts, *Ethics* (New York: Henry Holt and Company, 1908), p. 187.

95. John Dewey, *How We Think* (New York: Minton, Balch & Co., 1929), p. 287.

96. Dewey, *The Quest for Certainty*, p. 135

97. William James, *Psychology*, I, 316.

98. Dewey, *Human Nature and Conduct*, p. 330.

99. *Ibid.*, p. 331.

100. Dewey, *The Quest for Certainty*, p. 303.

101. *Ibid.*, p. 251.

102. Dewey, *Art as Experience*, p. 327.

103. *Ibid.*, p. 336.

104. Dewey, *The Quest for Certainty*, p. 273.

105. *Ibid.*   106. *Ibid.*, p. 274

107. *Ibid.*, pp. 88-91.

VI. INSTRUMENTATION IN RELIGIOUS EXPERIENCE

1. John Dewey, *Experience and Nature* (New York: W. W. Norton & Co., Inc., 1929), pp. 432-33.

2. *Ibid.*, pp. 436-37.   3. *Ibid.*, p. 410.

4. John Dewey, *The Quest for Certainty* (New York: Minton, Balch & Co., 1929), p. 255.

5. *Ibid.*, pp. 219-20.

6. Dewey, *Experience and Nature*, p. 407.

7. Dewey, *The Quest for Certainty*, p. 125.

8. *Ibid.*, p. 191.

9. John Dewey, *How We Think* (New York: Minton, Balch & Co., 1929), p. 136.

10. Dewey, *Experience and Nature*, p. 368.

11. John Dewey, *How We Think*, p. 138.

12. John Dewey, *Art as Experience* (New York: Minton, Balch & Co., 1934), p. 241.

13. *Ibid.*, pp. 319-20.   14. *Ibid.*, p. 273.

15. Dewey, *How We Think*, p. 142.

16. Dewey, *The Quest for Certainty*, p. 251.

17. *Ibid.*, p. 191.

18. John Dewey, *Human Nature and Conduct* (New York: Henry Holt & Company, 1922), pp. 259-60.

19. Dewey, *Experience and Nature*, p. 376.

20. Dewey, *The Quest for Certainty*, p. 275.

21. *Ibid.*,

22. John Dewey, *How We Think*, p. 87.

23. Dewey, *Experience and Nature*, p. 364.

24. *Ibid.*, p. 398.

25. Dewey, *The Quest for Certainty*, p. 268.

26. *Ibid.*, p. 37.

27. Dewey, *Experience and Nature*, p. 412.

28. John Dewey, *How We Think*, p. 63.

29. Dewey, *Human Nature and Conduct*, p. 166.

30. *Ibid.*, p. 167.

31. Dewey, *The Quest for Certainty*, p. 273.

32. This selection of data set forth in the narratives of

(Hebraic-Christian) Christian scriptures is not predicated upon any judgment as to their historicity but upon recognition of their wide acceptance as authentic didactic material. This is not to imply that the question of historicity is an indifferent issue but that for the specific intent of the argument it may be allowed to stand without prejudice. Whatever may have been the historic conditions out of which they were developed, the religious observances instituted in the Jewish and Christian traditions may be taken as instances in which experimental validation has been demonstrated.

33. Dewey, *Experience and Nature*, p. 263.

34. *Ibid.*, p. 270.

35. Dewey, *Art as Experience*, p. 30.

36. John Dewey, *How We Think*, p. 41.

37. *Ibid.*, p. 49.   38. *Ibid.*, pp. 224-25.

39. *Ibid.*, p. 19.

40. Dewey, *Art as Experience*, p. 329.

41. Dewey, *Experience and Nature*, p. 192.

42. *Ibid.*, p. 202.

43. At this point in the discussion, a "creed" is conceived on the basis of its function, when employed constructively in educational procedure. Some recognition of the use to which "creeds" were put in the history of the Christian Church is set forth later in this chapter. But here the artistic formulation of a creed as an instrumentality in the promotion of religious experience is taken as its primary meaning.

44. Dewey, *The Quest for Certainty*, pp. 154-55.

45. *Ibid.*, p. 194.   46. *Ibid.*, p. 218.

47. *Ibid.*, p. 277.

48. An interesting proposal is suggested by W. P. Montague in *Liberal Theology* (p. 159) that the modern church should retain two creeds, viz., "the creed of our cultural past" and "our present creed," the second to be held as a supplement to the first. Apparently his idea would be to appreciate the *esthetic* quality of the first, and the *artistic* quality of the second. He proposes, "The one creed will be *sung*, the other will be *said*." In such a procedure the historic creed could serve as a media-

tor of religious experience, as the carrier of a cultural heritage, that would be independent of the literal meaning of the words, whereas the contemporary creed could be used to set forth the present intellectual form of beliefs currently held.

49. Dewey, *The Quest for Certainty*, p. 277.

50. It is not denied that in the early history of the Christian Church famous creeds were developed as instrumentalities designed to set forth dogmatically such preferred cast of doctrine as would serve to screen the motley assembly of persons claiming to be Christians at a time of conflicting ideas as to the nature of what was to be believed. (Even so, that artificial use of creeds would have some indirect bearing upon education at that time.) However, throughout the argument of this discussion tautological interest has been focused upon the problem of "education in religion" as it would arise within the outlook of a confessional group. Thus the description here set forth of the nature and function of a creed is not so much based upon the testimony of the past as recorded by historians who may have had no definite interest in noting or understanding educational aspects in ancient events, as it is projected logically from ideas which are being examined in the course of this study.

VII: CONCLUSION

1. John Dewey, *Experience and Nature* (New York: W. W. Norton & Co., Inc., 1929), p. 405.

2. *Ibid.*, pp. 408-9.   3. *Ibid.*, pp. 115-16.

4. *Ibid.*, pp. 404-5.   5. *Ibid.*, p. 411.

6. *Ibid.*, p. 81.   7. *Ibid.*, p. 372.

8. *Ibid.*

9. John Dewey, *Art as Experience* (New York: Minton, Balch & Co., 1934), p. 79.

INDEX

Art, 135-49; as the implementation of social intercourse, 89; force most fully manifested in literature, 89; informs and shares culture, 113-14; transforms nature in objects, 140-43; incorporates all aspects in unity, 140; products are final, 141; products manifest "life of a civilization," 141; products may have "universal" character, 141; produces classic "symbols" for religion, 142; products have broad instrumental significance, 142-45; products equal to nature, 143; interwoven with science, 144; facilitates participation in culture, 145; intimate relation to mental activity, 146; promotes changes in character, 146; facilitates communication, 146; produces values, 147; facilitates communion, 147; products promote community, 148; serves education, 148; involved in processes of religion, 149; possibly causes resistance to change, 175; Miriam's song a product of art, 203-4; involved in production of significant instrumentalities in promotion of religion, 214; is nature transformed by entering new relationship, 235; in producing religious goods is geared into concrete actual situations, 238

Baptism, designed to perpetuate significance of commencement of Christian life, 205

Belief, 90-101; grounded in social process, 91; determines direction, 91; involves more than meaning, 91; refers beyond itself, 91; two modes of, 91-92; a third mode of, 93; more involved in concepts of persons, 93-94; content is about the eventual, 94; because artful no discount, 94-95; need not be operationally verified to produce values, 95-97; grounded in prior experience, 95; formed by individual choice, 96; involves man in consequence, 97; may be adopted, 97; intellectual responsibility important, 98; point beyond reach of empirical examination, 98; pragmatic examination possible by practice and logic, 99; logical examination produces creeds, 99; critical valuation